Praise for *Debt Cycle Investing*

"As a long-time Wall Streeter, I didn't think I could learn anything from a how-to-invest book. I was wrong!"—Barbara Steiner, founding partner, institutional research firm Portales Partners

"Original, well-argued, and meticulously supported—an important contribution to the literature on investing that all investors should read."—John Cecil, chairman, Eagle Knolls Capital, and former CFO, Lehman Brothers

"Helps us understand complex economic and market concepts in a straightforward manner with humor."—Steve Shapiro, former princpal, Concordia Capital Partners

"I've rarely seen information so convincingly presented—and so logically. Valuable and entertaining!"—Steve Rosenblatt, former IBM executive

Debt Cycle Investing

Debt Cycle Investing

Simple Tools for Reading the Economy

to Make Smarter Investment Decisions

Gary Gordon

WO STER

BOOKS

Printed in the United States of America

ISBN-13: 978-0692140055
ISBN-10: 0692140050
LCCN Imprint Name: Wooster Books

Wooster Books are available online from Amazon as well as from bookstores and other retailers. Orders and other correspondence may be addressed to:

Wooster Books
628 Orienta Avenue
Mamaroneck NY 10543
Email: jeeves0401@yahoo.com

Contents

Introduction: Financial Asset Allocation— The Basics and My New Idea

THIS IS A BOOK ABOUT INVESTING—a new addition to a vast library of existing books, all intended to help people like you grow your financial assets to secure a better retirement, a better education for your kids, the chance to buy a home or launch a business, and more.

Why a new book on such a well-trodden topic? Because I believe I have something unique to offer: an explanation of how the economy actually affects your investments, that you can easily understand and use to enhance your investment returns.

The relationship between the economy and your investments is an important topic, which is why mountains of newsprint, trillions of online pixels, and countless hours of broadcast time are devoted to it. Most people find this flood of expert commentary confusing, contradictory, and un-helpful. And in truth, most of it is. In the pages that follow, I'll explain my view of how the connection between the economy and investing *really* works and how you can use that knowledge to your financial advantage. I also help you keep up to date on the link between the economy and investing on my blog garygordoninvesting.com. Check it out.

The information in this book should help you more profitably *allocate* your investment assets—in other words, adjust your mix of financial assets over time to more likely achieve your personal financial goals.

Several asset classes make up the vast bulk of investments owned by Americans, as shown in Table I.1.

Table I.1. Asset classes owned by US investors at the end of 2017. (Source: Fed.)*

As of end of 2017	In $ trillions
Stocks	$40
Bonds	17
Bank deposits and money market funds	11
Real estate (my estimate)	5
Other (my estimate)	2
Total net worth	$75

Table I.1 shows that most of our investments are held in stocks, bonds, and "cash." In the investment world, the term *cash* includes far more than dollar bills and change. It also includes any assets that can be quickly and reliably converted to cash—bank deposits, certificates of deposit (CDs), money market funds, and US Treasury bills (the kind of US government debt that matures within a year).

Why is most of our money in stocks, bonds, and cash rather than real estate, pork belly futures, or Beanie Baby collectibles? For some excellent reasons. Stocks, bonds, and cash are all readily traded in huge markets, whose size is measured in tens of trillions of dollars. This means that investors can quickly and inexpensively buy and sell them, often with a few clicks of their smartphones. By comparison, real estate investments are expensive and time-consuming to buy and sell, and require time and money to manage. The same is true of most of the other assets you can invest in— fine art, antiques, and complex financial instruments like commodity futures. Sure, I love Beanie Babies—I'm not *completely* heartless—but it would be impractical to have half my assets invested in them. For these reasons, most investors are happy to hold the great bulk of their money in stocks, bonds, and cash.

---

* For an explanation of the data sources used here and in the tables and other figures throughout the book, see the list on pages 42-43.

To simplify our asset allocation discussion, I focus on one specific investment within each asset class:

- *For cash investments, a 1-year bank certificate of deposit (CD).* Bank deposits are by far the most popular cash investment held by US households.
- *For bonds, the 10-year Treasury bond.* Municipal bonds are actually households' biggest direct bond holding at 39% of the total. ("Direct" as opposed to an indirect bond investment held in a mutual fund or pension account.) But US Treasury bonds are second at 32%. And the correlation over time between municipal bond and Treasury bond yields is quite close, so analyzing their investment performance is pretty similar. Corporate bonds, another big bond holding, have some different characteristics from Treasuries, which I discuss later.
- *For stocks, the Standard & Poor's 500 index.* This index tracks the performance of 500 of the largest publicly traded companies in the US. The S&P 500 index is one of the most commonly used gauge for measuring how the stock market as a whole is doing. I'm sticking to the basics here.

If you're seeking tips about finding a hot stock that is sure to double in the next three weeks or making a mint on bitcoin, please look elsewhere.

Note that asset allocation focuses on "relative" return, not "absolute" return. For example, I may conclude that expected returns at a particular time are 5% for cash, 10% for bonds, and 15% for stocks. All of these returns are good, but stocks are the best of the lot and therefore would be overweighted in your portfolio.

The Three Traditional
Asset Allocation Decision Factors

LIKE MOST AMERICANS, you have probably already invested your financial assets in some mix of stocks, bonds, and cash. But what asset allocation mix is optimal for *you*?

To begin with, it's important to recognize that there is no single right answer to that question. But there are some useful rules of thumb. One is the so-called 60/40 Rule, which says to put 60% of your money into stocks, 40% into bonds. Another is the Rule of 100, which recommends that you subtract your age from 100 and put that percentage in stocks. For example, using the Rule of 100, a 70-year-old investor should have 30% of her investment money in stocks, the rest in bonds and cash.

But we are all different, with different circumstances and needs. Therefore, the rules of thumb are only starting points. Three personal factors widely recognized as playing a crucial role in individuals' investment asset allocation weightings are *time, income needs, and risk tolerance.*

Factor One: Time

WHAT IS YOUR PERSONAL INVESTMENT TIME HORIZON? That is, how long do you have until you plan to spend your savings? It could be six months for a vacation, three years for a down payment on a home, 15 years until your kids head to college, or 30 years until retirement. The longer your time horizon, the more your asset allocation should be tilted toward stocks. The reason is that stock investments have delivered higher returns over the long term than bonds or cash. I calculate that since 1960 stocks earned investors 12% a year on average, versus 7% for bonds and 5% for cash.

In the short term, however, stocks can be very volatile, rising or falling unexpectedly. During 2008, for instance, the S&P 500 index declined by 37%. At one point during the depths of the Depression in 1932, stocks were down a shocking 62% year-over-year. But the longer you have to invest, the more likely you are to get average returns. For example, during the worst ten-year period for stocks since 1960, their average return was only down 2%. Even the disastrous 1932 losses were nearly recovered in full within two years.

So if you are investing for a goal that is many years in the future, you can afford to ride out the ups and downs of the stock market—and over that long time period, stocks will almost certainly give you a better return than bonds or cash. But if your time horizon is shorter, you want to put more money into bonds or cash, giving up a higher possible return in exchange for less volatility and therefore less short-term risk that the money won't be there when you need it.

Suppose, for example, you're 25 and have just landed your dream job with the Mafia. The mob's 401(k) retirement plan allows you to save up to 10% of your extortion income, which the syndicate matches. You expect to be out of prison in time to retire at age 65. Since you have a 40-year investment time horizon, you should heavily overweight stocks when allocating your investment funds.

On the other hand, suppose that you've been saving for a house for the last five years and at last you have the down payment. You're calling a realtor tomorrow. Your investment time frame is therefore a matter of months. That means you can't afford a 15% stock market correction. Your asset allocation should be heavily weighted towards cash.

Factor Two: Income Needs

THE SECOND FACTOR YOU NEED TO CONSIDER when making asset allocation choices is your need for current income from your investments. Generally, investors should focus on *total return*. This is the sum of asset appreciation—that is, the growth in value of your investment—plus income from interest and dividends. But if you rely on your investments to pay your monthly bills, you will want to lean towards those investments that pay you regular cash returns, like bonds, cash, and dividend-paying stocks.

Classically, retirees need to focus more on current income and less on asset appreciation, while working stiffs can structure their portfolios to achieve the highest potential long-term total return, in which asset appreciation plays a larger role.

Factor Three: Risk Management

THEORETICALLY, A GROUP OF PEOPLE OF THE SAME AGE, income, and savings should have the same asset allocation. Yet in reality these people will probably choose a range of allocations, in large part based on their tolerance for risk.

Several factors affect the degree of risk associated with managing your investments.

- *Your level of diversification.* The more individual stocks and bonds you own, the less volatile your returns will be. For example, owning 100 of the S&P 500 stocks means your returns will fairly closely mirror the S&P 500 index. However, owning just four stocks risks much wider swings in your investment performance. As an example, during 2017, the S&P 500 index rose by 18%. To compare, I used Excel's random number generator to pick four large stocks. Chevron rose by 18% last year, Cisco by 30%, Johnson & Johnson by 28%, and United Technologies by 20%, for an average of 24%. Two lessons. First, Excel's random number generator is great at picking stocks! Second, less diversification means wider swings in return. How wide are the swings you can afford to tolerate?
- *The riskiness of your individual investments.* For example, in 2014, oil company stock prices were hit by a decline in oil prices. Suppose in 2014 I'd invested in oil giant Exxon, which has a global and diversified oil-related business and modest debt. I would have sustained a 20% loss between April 1, 2014, and October 3,

2017. Or I could have bought Chesapeake Energy, a US-based driller with loads of debt. Its stock price fell by 84% over the same period. It's possible Chesapeake will be a lot more fun to own if the price of oil shoots up again, but you can see the greater risk involved in Chesapeake's stock as compared with Exxon's. Are you attracted to (relatively low risk) blue chips or to (higher risk) penny stocks?

- *The amount of trading.* Active stock traders optimistically believe that they can identify short-term trading opportunities that may exist for as short as a few days or even hours. Evidence suggests, however, that they are usually wrong. As I note below, studies have shown that active traders generally earn less than buy-and-hold investors. What's more, each trade generates a commission expense, so active trading is more costly to maintain than a buy-and-hold strategy. Are you working your Schwab account every day? Or do you just check in once a month?

- *Your patience level.* I'll illustrate with an example of my own costly impatience. Facebook went public in 2012 at $33 per share. I can't remember exactly why, but the stock quickly dropped to $18. I swooped in and bought some shares. The stock then quickly rose, making me feel like a genius. I locked in my gain by selling my shares at about $25. The price of Facebook shares now? As of May 7, 2018, $178. I got the first seven points, but through my impatience I lost the next 153. Would you still be holding on to the stock?

These four investment risk factors can be summarized as measures of your *level of investment confidence.* For this insight, I am indebted to a panel recently put together by UBS, including Svetlana Gherzi, Ph.D., UBS; Terry Odean, professor at the University of California at Berkeley; Dennis Ruhl, JP Morgan Asset Management; and Michael Crook, UBS. The panelists made the point that overconfidence and underconfidence are two of the main sources of poor asset allocation and weak investment results.

In their article "Trading Can Be Hazardous to Your Wealth" (*Journal of Finance*, April, 2000), Brad Barber and Terry Odean put it this way:

> Individual investors who hold common stocks directly pay a tremendous performance penalty for active trading. Of 66,465 households with accounts at a large discount broker during 1991 to 1996, those that trade most earn an annual return of 11.%, while the market returns 17.9%. The average household earns an annual return of 16.4% . . . Overconfidence can explain high trading levels and the resulting poor performance of individual investors.

Underconfidence—the evil twin of overconfidence—can similarly weaken your investment results. For example, an underconfident investor will hold too much cash and bonds and shy away from stocks, despite the higher average returns that stocks provide over time. He will also tend to follow the herd, assuming that others must know better—even when the choices of the herd are inappropriate for him. Both over- and under-confidence tend to distract us from the asset allocation choices that are best for us.

Two factors can combat investing overconfidence or underconfidence. One is to adhere to those asset allocation rules of thumb, which favors reason over emotion. The other is to seek out and rely on facts. Jim Simons, the founder of Renaissance Technologies, a wildly successful hedge fund that pioneered big data investing, put it this way in a *New Yorker* magazine article:

> Renaissances's methods are proprietary and secret—but he did share with [the article's author D.T. Max] the key to his investing success: he "never overrode the model." Once he settled on what should happen, he held tight until it did.

In fact, I argue for fact-finding as a profitable fourth asset allocation factor.

My Fourth Factor: Fact-Based Asset Reallocation

TIME, INCOME NEEDS AND RISK MANAGEMENT are fundamental realities that every financial advisor should review with you in setting your asset allocation. This book adds a fourth factor—fact-based asset *re-allocation* based on changes in relative asset values.

The underlying concept is simple. Sometimes one asset class gets unusually cheap or expensive in comparison to the others. These major mispricings don't come along often, but when they do, taking advantage of them can make a big difference in your long-term returns.

Recognizing these occasional mispricings isn't easy. To help you identify them, this book offers you three tools. The first is charts that present financial information in a form that's easy to understand and learn from. The second is an asset valuation tool I call the *earnings yield model*. It can spot for you when assets are cheap or expensive. The third tool is understanding *the debt growth cycle*, which I will show plays a major role in driving economic and investment cycles.

The debt growth cycle? What does that have to do with investing? You don't read about it in the media, you don't hear about it at cocktail parties. But this book will show you that identifying and acting upon the debt growth cycle can give you a meaningful long-term performance edge over other investors, even that jerk at work who's always bragging about his latest hot tech stock.

This book won't help you predict every market wiggle. No system can explain, much less anticipate, small movements of the markets. This truth underlies the warnings most wise investment advisors make about the folly of trying to "time the market." Instead, tracking the debt growth cycle helps you to identify and take advantage of times when stocks, bonds, or cash are *materially* undervalued or overvalued.

When undervaluations occur, you make extra money by shifting your allocation towards that asset class at their low prices and waiting for those prices to rebound—as they almost invariably do. When overvaluations occur, you can benefit by shifting away from those assets. You can benefit even more from overvaluation by using investment techniques like *short selling*, which let you profit from a decline in the value of an asset.

Investing attracts many of America's best and brightest because so much money is at stake. All are avidly searching for asset mispricings. When they believe they've spotted one, they jump on it, which limits and then eliminates the under- or overvaluation. So how can any investment asset stay cheap or expensive enough, for long enough, for little people like you and me to take advantage of the valuation anomaly? Aren't those hedge fund billionaires scooping up those mispriced assets before you and I have had our morning coffee and played our usual 30 Candy Crush games?

Maybe so. An academic theory called the *efficient market* theory says that nobody can predict future returns better than the next person, so attempts to identify investments that are temporarily undervalued or overvalued are basically futile.

But the fact is that stocks, bonds, or cash *do* get mispriced for long enough for even ordinary investors to benefit from them. Legendary investor Jeremy Grantham noted this in his third quarter 2017 investor letter for his GMO investment fund letter:

> [Individual] stocks are getting more efficiently priced . . . Asset classes are absolutely not . . . In 2007-08 there was the broadest overpricing [of stocks] across all countries, over 1 standard deviation, than there had ever been. So, major opportunities at the asset class level have been alive and well in this period of the last 20 years . . .

To quantify the frequency of these investment extremes, I measured annualized results for stocks, bonds, and cash in three-year periods starting in 1960, as follows:

- For stocks, I assumed the purchase of an S&P 500 index fund at the start of each three-year period. I summed dividend payments made over the following three years, then added the gain or loss as if the index was sold three years later.
- For bonds, I assumed the purchase of a ten-year Treasury bond at the start of each three-year period, summing three years of the interest rate prevailing at the start, then added the gain or loss on the assumed sale of the bond after three years.
- For cash, I assumed three consecutive purchases of 1-year CDs.

As expected, over the long run stocks outperformed bonds and cash. But I also discovered significant anomalies—periods when the "normal" relationship among the big three asset classes did *not* hold true.

- Cash or bonds beat stocks 36% of the time.
- Stocks lost money 13% of the time.
- Cash was the best performing asset during the entire decade of the 1970s.
- Bonds significantly outperformed stocks and cash following both the Internet bubble (from 2000 through 2002) and the housing bubble (from 2006 through 2008).

Trying to recognize unusual time periods that provide similar opportunities therefore seems like a worthwhile goal—especially now, in 2018, because *the US, and to a large extent the globe, is currently experiencing two investment extremes.*

Most people don't realize that these extremes exist. The return to actual normalcy, when it occurs—as it almost inevitably will—should therefore be a big surprise to investors. Figure I.1 shows the two economic trends that are driving today's investment extremes.

Figure I.1. Two current investment extremes: An unusually high level of debt outstanding, and an unusually low interest rate policy on the part of the major country central banks, including the Federal Reserve. (Sources: Total debt and federal funds rate—Fed. GDP—BEA.)

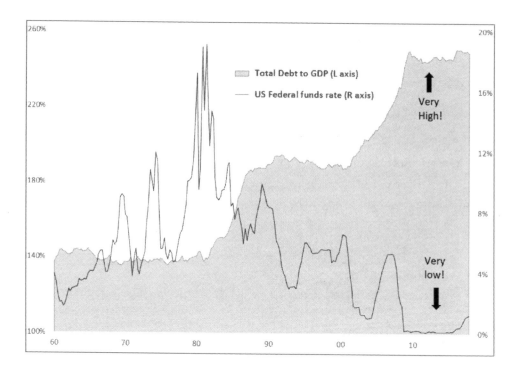

For now, you don't have to fully grasp the messages of Figure I.1; I delve into these issues in detail later in the book. You just have to notice that the ratio of total debt to gross domestic product (GDP) has never been higher than it is today, while the fed funds interest rate is extraordinarily low. These two facts have big implications for financial markets—implications that most investors today generally ignore.

Explaining how you can recognize investment extremes when they occur, and how to use this understanding to make smarter asset allocation decisions, is the core purpose of this book

1 Our All-Too-Human Investment Weaknesses

IT MIGHT SEEM ODD that investment extremes are not routinely factored into the asset allocation decisions made by investors. No one needs any special advice or training to notice when the temperature falls below freezing or approaches the 100-degree mark. Why doesn't the same apply to investment extremes?

Many experts believe that investment extremes are difficult to recognize. For example, the former Federal Reserve chairman Alan Greenspan famously said in a speech on August 30, 2002, "It was very difficult to definitively identify a bubble until after the fact—that is, when its bursting confirmed its existence."

With all due respect to the former Fed chairman, I strongly disagree. Financial bubbles are *easy* to spot. What is hard is to *emotionally accept* their existence. The fact is, we humans are flawed. (Okay, not Beyoncé, but everyone else.) We have trouble understanding complexity. We don't grasp statistical concepts very well. We prefer stories to facts.

Daniel Kahneman and Amos Tversky were pioneers in identifying some of the common weaknesses in human economic thinking. Their work established the field of behavioral economics. They are now far from alone. In fact, Richard Thaler won the 2017 Nobel Prize in Economics for, as *The Wall Street Journal* put it, "upending the notion that people make rational decisions about their futures and finances." Understanding these weaknesses can help you to recognize them in yourself. In this chapter, I describe five crucial weaknesses, as laid out in Kahneman's book, *Thinking Fast and Slow* (Farrar Straus, 2013). Note that my examples of these weaknesses generally relate to the housing market, especially its boom and bust during the

2000s. That's because I worked as a stock analyst covering the housing and mortgage industries, so I flatter myself that I know something about the topic. In addition, I've maintained a data base covering the housing market even into my retirement, which is both lucky for you and a sad commentary about me.

We Fall for Stories

KAHNEMAN REFERS TO THE HUMAN TENDENCY to embrace compelling stories—even those that are logically flawed—as *the narrative fallacy*. He writes, "Narrative fallacies arise inevitably from our continuous attempt to make sense of the world. The explanatory stories that people find compelling are simple; are concrete; assign a larger role to talent, stupidity, and intentions than to luck; and focus on a few striking events that happened rather than on the countless events that failed to happen" (*Thinking Fast and Slow*, page 199).

Economic stories that match Kahneman's description arise all of the time. When millions of people—including smart people and supposed experts—believe these stories, they become powerful enough to affect society's behavior, including the prices they are willing to pay for financial assets. Thus, these stories help to create financial asset pricing bubbles and to sustain them beyond the point at which you might assume they'd be obvious to everyone.

An expensive economic story popular during the early 2000s developed around home prices, based on the data in Figure 1.1. The story went, "Home prices never go down. After all, there's only so much land, and God isn't making any more of it. So smart people invest in houses, because you can never lose by doing that."

Figure 1.1. A dangerous fable: "Home prices never go down." And they essentially hadn't since the Great Depression . . . until the 2008 housing crash. (Source: Fed, Census.)

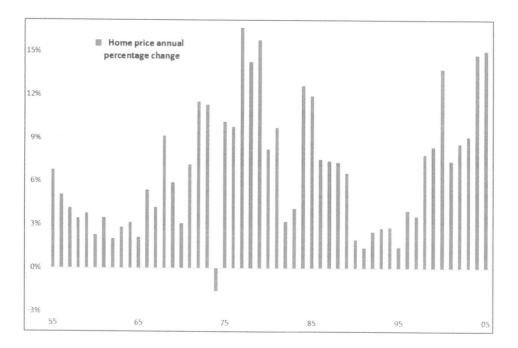

The picture shows that national home prices declined in only one year in the 50 years prior to 2006—a 50-year period that included eight recessions, when prices of lots of other assets, such as stocks, had plummeted for periods of time. And even that single year of decline was sandwiched between two increases of 10% or more. So by the mid-2000s, the story that home prices never go down was widely believed, not only by average citizens but even by housing professionals who make their living building houses and making home loans.

For example, here's a comment from 2006 by Robert Toll, then-CEO of homebuilder Toll Brothers: "The next great story is pent-up demand . . . Once the natural balance is restored in the market, you're going to see prices go up again. Prices are going to go up quite a bit" (Associated Press, June 6, 2006).

And here's one from the same year from an executive with New Century Financial, then the #10 mortgage lender in the US and the #2 sub-prime lender (that is, a lender that makes loans to those with weak credit histories): "Isolated difficult markets, but do not expect widespread prop-erty value declines . . . *However, expect our credit performance to be within modeled and reserved levels*" (Southern California Investor Conference, August 11, 2006, my italics).

Most other "experts" agreed that sky-high home prices would continue to rise. After all, didn't everyone "know" the story that home prices never go down?

The appeal of a story where only good things happen—"Home prices never go down"—is obvious. But when the story is not true, it leads to really stupid economic and investing behavior. On the homebuilding side, it led to the construction of two million empty housing units by 2007. On the mortgage lending side, it drove the volume of risky subprime lending from $150 billion in 2000 to over $600 billion in 2005.

Of course, the home price fable didn't have a happy ending. Housing prices started to decline in late 2006. By 2008, the bubble had burst. From 2006 to 2010, Toll Brothers' home sales declined by 69%, the company lost over $1 billion from 2007 to 2010, and Toll's stock price plummeted from a high of $59 per share in 2005 to $16 in 2011. And within seven months of the rosy prediction offered by the New Century executive, his company had declared bankruptcy. Followed by the bankruptcies of nine of the top 20 mortgage lenders. Followed by the seizure of giant mortgage insurers Fannie Mae and Freddie Mac by the US government. Fannie Mae's stock price dove from $65 in mid-2007 to a microscopic $0.33 in 2011. As we MBAs put it, not good.

Clearly, identifying popular economic fables and recognizing the risks they conceal can create significant added value for investors.

We Believe Humans Are Largely
Rational Economic Beings

AN ASSUMPTION UNDERLYING MOST ECONOMIC ANALYSIS is that free market participants behave in a logical, self-interested manner. And even if it is conceded that some of us occasionally act irrationally, it is argued that as a group we are steely-eyed rationalists. Kahneman cites a sentence from a paper on economic theory that neatly summarizes this assumption: "The agent of economic theory is rational, selfish, and his tastes do not change." Kahnemen recalls being "astonished" at this assertion. "To a psychologist," Kahneman writes, "it is self-evident that people are neither fully rational nor completely selfish, and that their tastes are anything but stable" (*Thinking Fast and Slow*, page 269).

You don't have to be a professional psychologist to know that people aren't fully rational. Any episode of *Real Housewives of Beverly Hills* makes that clear. So why do so many economists make that assumption?

Here's the likely reason. Dictionary.com defines economics as "The science that deals with the production, distribution, and consumption of goods and services, or the material welfare of humankind." Note the word *science* in this definition. You can't create a science around irrational actions. Physics is a science because gravity *always* works; we call it the "law" of gravity. Mathematics is a science because 5 + 4 *always* equals 9. So economists who want to be considered scientists *need* to assume that people are *always* rational and selfish, with tastes that *never* change. As a result, many economists indulge in the wishful thinking that economic behavior is far more predictable and consistent than it really is.

Here's an example drawn from an economics textbook, *Macroeconomics*, by Robert J. Gordon (no relation to me, luckily for him). Don't worry about understanding the details. Just notice the importance of the two words *assumed* and *regarded* (my italics):

The most important macroeconomic model developed by classical economists is the famous "quantity equation," relating the nominal money supply (M) and velocity (V) to the price level (P) and real GDP (Y). MV = PY . . . To convert the quantity equation into a theory, classical economists *assumed* that any change in M or V in the left side of the equation would be balanced by a proportional change in P on the right-hand side of the equation, with no change in real GDP (Y) . . . Velocity was *regarded* as being relatively stable . . .

Notice what the classical economists described by Professor Gordon did. They did not base their crucial "quantity equation" on any evidence from the real world—the kind of evidence that physicists, for example, rely on. Instead, they simply "assumed" that certain relationships are true, and "regarded" the money supply velocity as "relatively stable." In other words, they just made stuff up. The result: an impressive-looking equation that allows economists to regard themselves as scientists, just like the physicists down the hall. And, as I will show you in chapter seven, they were dead wrong.

Making up economic equations based on assumptions rather than any actual facts is a harmless activity—until you start making real-world predictions and decisions based upon them. To the extent that we can limit our reliance on these assumptions, our investment results will benefit.

Figure 1.2 presents more evidence that we humans are not as rational as we like to think. I didn't label it, so you can focus on the wild swings in the data, which seem far more emotional than cold-bloodedly logical. Quick guess about what the graph represents?

Figure 1.2. This chart captures far more emotion than logic. What is it? (Source: Not telling.)

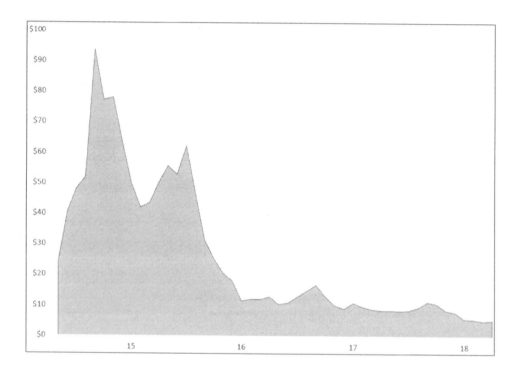

Okay, I'll end the excruciating suspense. It's the stock price chart for camera-maker GoPro. When I first became aware of GoPro's products, they struck me as novelty items for self-absorbed skiers and mountain bikers. The *real* camera product was the ubiquitous smartphone in our pockets. Yet many investors got caught up in the emotional hype, sending the value of the company at peak to a dazzling $10 billion. Today GoPro is losing money, and its valuation is down to $750 million. Which still seems high, but I won't go there.

We Assume That Today's Trend
Is Likely to Continue Indefinitely

WHEN WE OBSERVE SOMETHING HAPPENING in the world around us, we tend to assume it will keep on happening. This trend-thinking comes naturally to us humans. It probably started with our distant ancestors: "The antelopes were by that watering hole yesterday, so they should be there today." The problem is that trend-thinking often flies in the face of reality. Things often change, and often without us being able to explain why. Why did hipsters take up weird beards and porkpie hats? Why did bellbottoms come and go? What is it about bitcoin that makes people lose their minds? I don't know, either.

In fact, most phenomena are governed by the concept of *regression to the mean*. *Mean* is another word for *average*, and regression to the mean implies that, over time, any behavior will vary around an average. For example, flip a coin four times and it's possible you might end up with four straight heads. Is heads more likely on flip number five? No—for any single coin flip, the chance of flipping a head is always the same, 50%. If you keep flipping the coin—ten times, then 100 times, then 1,000 times—the percentage of heads will gravitate closer and closer to 50%. Similarly, if you are an 18-handicap golfer but shoot a seven over par today, the odds are that you will shoot a lot closer to 18 over par next time (sorry, but it's true).

Kahneman notes that we humans tend to resist the concept of regression to the mean: "Whether undetected or wrongly explained, the phenomenon of regression is strange to the human mind. So strange, indeed, that it was first identified and understood two hundred years after the theory of gravitation and differential calculus" (*Thinking Fast and Slow*, page 179).

I've frequently seen how the concept of regression to the mean is ignored during extreme economic conditions. Instead, the extreme becomes anchored as normal in peoples' minds if it lasts long enough, leading them to think that today's conditions are likely to persist indefinitely.

The home price roller coaster of the 2000s highlights this misperception very clearly. Let's start with Figure 1.3.

Figure 1.3. Home price increases soared above household income increases during the housing bubble of the 2000s—until regression to the mean kicked in. (Sources: Household income—Census. Home prices—Federal Housing Finance Agency.)

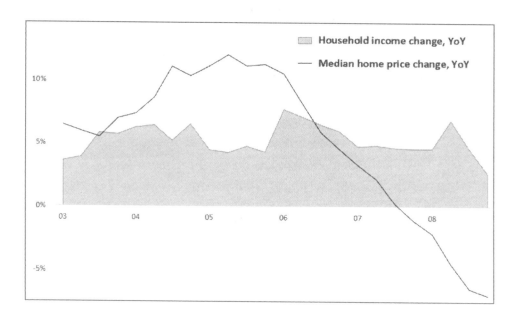

The figure shows the wild swing in annual home prices, from increases greater than 10% during 2004-2006 to a decrease in 2008, a downtrend that lasted into 2012. The graph also shows changes in household income, because household income is an excellent benchmark, or mean, against which to measure home price increases. Rationally, you'd expect that, in the long term, home prices will rise only as fast as buyers' ability to pay. In other words, you should expect average home price increases over time to regress to the mean of household income growth.

Yet in fact peoples' expectations frequently defy the logic of regression to the mean. I remember vividly a survey that the economist at the financial services firm UBS did when I worked there in early 2005, when home prices were booming. He surveyed UBS wealth management customers on a variety of financial and economic questions, including how much they expected home prices to increase over the following five years. These surveyed customers certainly were richer than average and almost assuredly better educated than average. So what was their average response?

These investors expected home prices to grow by *12%* annually for five years—more than double the growth predicted by regression to the mean. The actual result? Over those five years home prices *fell* by 0.5% annually. And the median home sale price fell by 28% from its peak in July, 2006 to its bottom in February, 2010. Investors, not just homeowners, shared in the pain of the regression to the mean. The stock market as a whole fell by 21% during that period. Mortgage insurance company MGIC fell by 86%.

Regression to the mean is an almost universal phenomenon. I promise that recognizing this reality will improve your asset allocation decisions.

We Cling to Our Favorite Theories

A LITTLE EARLIER, I HAD A BIT OF FUN mocking the pseudo-scientific underpinnings of some economic theory. But the truth is that, over the years, most of us have absorbed some economic theory, first-hand (from classes or textbooks) or second-hand (from pundits, politicians, or financial advisors). And this inevitably distorts our observations and thinking about real-world economics. In Kahneman's words, "Once you have accepted a theory and used it as a tool in your thinking, it is extraordinarily difficult to notice its flaws. If you come upon an observation that does not seem to fit the model, you assume that there must be a perfectly good explanation that you are

somehow missing. You give the theory the benefit of the doubt . . . "
(*Thinking Fast and Slow*, page 277).

Economic theories rooted in political beliefs are particularly insidious
in their ability to trample facts because of the large emotional commitments
people often make in them. For example, one popular political belief is that
when something goes wrong in the economy, the government must be at
fault. An economic corollary is the theory that business people are too
rational to do anything really stupid.

A common stock market theory is the *first mover advantage*. For example,
from *The Motley Fool* on December 7, 2017: "Will there be a significant 'first-
mover' advantage in self-driving cars? Will the first company (or group of
companies) to bring the technology to market enjoy significant long-term
advantages over rivals that lag?"

FitBit was the first mover in the "activity tracker" category. (Actually,
the KGB was pretty good at it too, but they didn't commercialize their
service.) So when investors got a crack at FitBit's stock, they went insane
with excitement. As Website Investor Place reported it, "The Fitbit IPO
priced Wednesday at $20 per share to top its expected range of $17 to $19,
which itself was lifted after an initial range of $14 to $16. And on top of all
that, the number of shares offered in the Fitbit IPO was increased from 29.9
million to 36.6 million. FIT stock followed up that performance with an early
spike of roughly 50% when shares debuted Thursday." The stock shortly
reached $48.

FitBit's first mover advantage followed on the heels of other companies
similarly first to the gate:

- The first mass-produced car: The Haynes Motor Car Company
- The first mass-produced PC: The Osborne Computer Company
- And who can forget the first social network: Friendster?

And first mover FitBit? The stock has been holding at $5 a share. Maybe
that first mover theory has a hole or two in it.

And here's my obligatory housing story to explain the problem with theories. What caused the housing bubble and bust of the 2000s? One theory would drive us toward the belief that, somehow, government must have been to blame. Former New York Mayor Michael Bloomberg nicely summed up this view: "It was not the banks that created the mortgage crisis. It was, plain and simple, Congress who forced everybody to go and give mortgages to people who were on the cusp . . . They were the ones who pushed Fannie and Freddie to make a bunch of loans that were imprudent, if you will" (*Forbes*, November 22, 2011).

If your theory is that the government always screws things up, this *has* to be the right explanation. But it's a fable. The facts are well summarized by Steve Denning, the author of the same *Forbes* story:

> It is clear to anyone who has studied the financial crisis of 2008 that the private sector's drive for short-term profit was behind it. More than 84% of the sub-prime mortgages in 2006 were issued by private lending . . . Out of the top 25 subprime lenders in 2006, only one was subject to the usual mortgage laws and regulations. The nonbank underwriters made more than 12 million subprime mortgages with a value of nearly $2 trillion. The lenders who made these were exempt from federal regulations.

If you need more evidence, read *The Big Short* by Michael Lewis (Norton, 2011), or watch the awesome 2015 movie. It details the irrational and often fraudulent behavior of mortgage lenders, mortgage investors, credit rating agencies, and yes, millions of borrowers during that time period.

Or ask me. As I've said, I was a Wall Street stock analyst then, and I saw the bubble and the collapse unfold close up. I followed home mortgage lenders like Countrywide Credit and IndyMac, watching how they shifted from low-profit government-insured mortgages to much higher profit subprime and Alt-A "liar loans" (so called because they required less—or no!— documentation of income and assets, and therefore were prone to fraud and abuse). I saw government agencies Fannie Mae, Freddie Mac, and the Federal Housing Administration (FHA) lose huge amounts of market share to their private-sector competitors in 2004 and 2005, as the subprime and liar loan bubble was peaking. I saw nearly all non-bank home mortgage lenders go bust, while the government-run FHA never did. And while Fannie Mae and Freddie Mac were placed into government conservatorship—the equivalent of bankruptcy—they not only paid back all of their government bailout money, they generated an $87 billion profit to us taxpayers to date (March, 2018).

None of these facts fit the "government is always wrong" theory, so many believers simply ignore the facts.

What's *your* favorite economic theory? Beware—whatever it is, it may be blinding you to some realities about how our world actually works. If you can take those blinders off, you will become a better investor.

I'll end this section on a classy note. I have a bone to pick with Ralph Waldo Emerson. He was a Transcendentalist, which meant he believed that all truths came from within. He derisively said (I quote from *Man's Better Angels* by Philip Gura), "The great majority of men [are] unable to judge of any principle until its light falls upon a fact…" Sorry, Ralphie boy, but I'm one of those men. Facts over theories. Emerson may have been a great poet, but I bet he was a stinky investor.

We Are Swayed in Our Thinking by Anchor Numbers

ONE OF THE WEIRDEST WEAKNESSES IN OUR ECONOMIC THINKING is our tendency to be excessively influenced by *anchor numbers*—the first figures, whatever they may be, that we encounter when considering a particular issue. As Kahneman observes, "Anchoring makes us far more suggestible than most of us would want to be" (*Thinking Fast and Slow*, page 126).

Here's a fun example cited by Kahneman. When students are asked how old the Indian leader Mohandas K. Gandhi was when he died, most have no idea. But when the question is posed, "Was Gandhi more than 114 years old when he died?" they tend to give quite high estimates—much higher than when they are asked, "Was Gandhi more than 35 years old when he died?" (For the record, Gandhi was 78 years old when he was assassinated in 1948.)

I've found that many people base their economic views on the latest data point they see in the media or on Twitter. For example, consider the fed funds rate, a key benchmark interest rate. In February, 2017, the fed funds rate stood at 0.7%. On February 23, Bankrate.com published a story containing this comment: "The Federal Reserve dropped the week's biggest bit of economic news when it released the minutes of its most recent monetary policy meeting. It seemed to hint that the Fed could increase short-term interest rates [to 1.0%] as early as its next meeting, in mid-March."

With the anchor at 0.7%, going to 1.0% may seem like "the week's biggest bit of economic news," as the news story put it. But look at the long-term history of the fed funds rate, shown in Figure 1-4 on the next page.

The chart makes clear that the 0.7% rate was remarkably low, and that an increase of just three-tenths of a percent to 1.0% is little more than a rounding error in the grand sweep of history. So the 0.7% anchor gives a misleading view of the significance of current Federal Reserve policy changes.

When considering any trend that is measured by numbers, try to put those numbers in the broadest possible context. Otherwise, you may be unduly influenced by the most recent number you've seen, which is unlikely to be particularly representative or significant.

Figure 1.4. With an anchor of 0%, going from 0.7% to above 1% seems like a big deal. But when you use the actual historical range of the fed funds rate as your anchor, an increase to 1% is revealed as minuscule. (Source: Fed.)

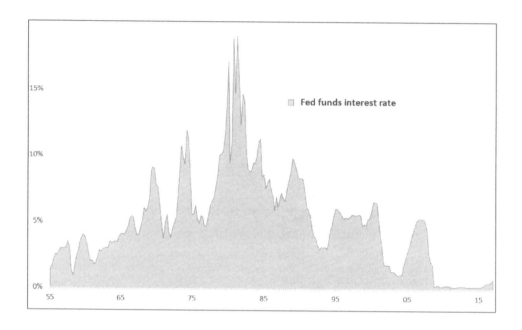

We Look for Confirmation That
Our Past Decisions Were Right

THIS DESCRIPTION COMES VIA DAN ARIELY (a follower of Kahnemann and Tversky) and Jeff Kreisler, in their book *Dollars and Sense*:

> When we've made a particular financial decision in the past, we tend to assume we've made the best decision possible. We look for data that supports our opinion, feeling even better about the quality of our decision.

This tendency, called *confirmation bias*, makes it hard to change our minds, and in the context of this book, our asset allocation. I saw confirmation bias at work all of the time during my career as a stock analyst. The first example is myself. While I was studying a stock for the first time, I believe I was reasonably objective. But once I put an official Buy or Sell rating on the stock, confirmation bias set in. The next piece of data was darn tootin' going to agree with my rating, even if I had to apply pretzel logic.

Similarly, I believe that my main value as a stock analyst for my clients was that I provided confirmation bias. If they owned Stock A, they were going to like me if I said that I agreed with them. And woe to me if I disagreed. I vividly remember a colleague who many years ago had the audacity to put a sell on most of the stocks in his industry. He turned out to be dead right. His reward? A far lower ranking from clients as compared with his peers.

Finally, another one on me. I take great pride in having forecast the 2008 financial crisis. The daily feedback telling me how smart I was felt good. I was therefore blind to the bottoming of the stock market in the spring of 2009, despite new facts about lower stock prices and massive support from the government and the Federal Reserve. I therefore I didn't take nearly enough advantage of the stock market rally that followed.

~

IT'S ABUNDANTLY CLEAR that everyone is prone to irrational lapses in judgment when thinking about economics. Even me. Shocking but true. The big question is: Can you limit these psychological mistakes, and make smarter financial decisions as a result?

I firmly believe that you can. Beginning in the next chapter, I'll show you how.

2 A Tool for Clearer Thinking: Pictures of Real Data

IN MY YEARS AS AN INVESTMENT ANALYST, I've found that I could overcome some of my weaknesses in economic thinking by relying on two tools:

- Pictures that capture actual economic data. Real data help ground you in reality, and visual presentations of those facts tell you more than statistics.
- An investment valuation model. This tool helps you identify and act on real investment values, thereby limiting trend-thinking, wishful thinking, and so on.

In this chapter, I review the first tool—visual representations of real economic data. I've already presented a few charts of economic statistics to illustrate points. Now let me explain my approach to chart-making and analysis.

Let's start with a not-quite-random economic question. Of course, it's a housing question. Suppose I want to forecast the growth of home mortgage debt. I could rely on an anchor, like last's quarter's growth rate, or I could assume that US homeowners are rational beings who only borrow as much as they can afford. Or I could look at a pictorial history of home mortgage debt to see how homeowners actually borrow. Let's choose the last option.

Then I ask what other piece of economic data might help to explain the actual changes in home mortgage debt growth. Changes in home prices come to mind. Is there a clear, consistent correlation between the two? To answer this question, I created Figure 2.1.

Figure 2.1. An example of how my charts are designed. (Sources: Mortgage debt—Fed. Home prices—Federal Housing Finance Agency.)

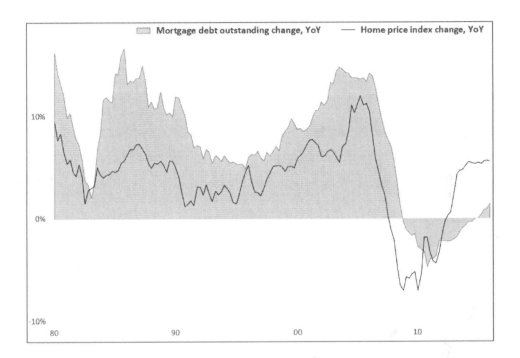

Let's review the features of Figure 2.1, because the charts throughout this book are designed along the same lines.

- A summary of the chart appears in the title. This is my interpretation of the significance of the data shown in the chart. It's possible that your view could differ! Don't be shy about questioning my analysis. I'm godlike only in my own mind.
- The data I use comes from reputable sources. In this case, the home mortgage data is from the Federal Reserve, and the home price data is from the Federal Housing Finance Agency (FHFA).

Both are government agencies with little incentive that I can see to bias the data.

- I use a solid area to display the data I am trying to explain, and a line to display the data I am testing as an explanation. So in Figure 2.1, the solid area is actual home mortgage debt growth, and the line is actual home price changes.

- The legends briefly define the data presented. Note that I frequently use annual or year-over-year (YoY) measurements.

- The scale of the data measurement appears along the left-hand vertical axis (the Y axis, as you may recall from high school math class). In Figure 2.1, the data being measured is YoY changes in both home mortgage debt and home prices, and the scale runs from -15% to +20%. If the relevant scales are very different for the two data sets, I use the left vertical axis for the area chart (the data being analyzed) and the right vertical axis for the line (the potential driver of the data being analyzed). Very often, as in this case, the scales aren't very important in themselves. All I want from this chart is to see whether there is a relationship between the two data sets, which is also called a *correlation*.

- The time period for the data measurement appears on the horizontal scale, or the X axis. In this chart, I measure the data from 1976 to the present. Note that I skip the centuries and the millennia, so "1980" is shown as "80." Again, the dates may not be very important if I am just testing for correlation. Also note that the more data I add to the chart, the harder it is to read, so I sometimes make the editorial judgment to exclude repetitive data from earlier years. And I argue later in the book that the US's economic dynamics changed materially after 1980, so my charts frequently start then.

I then analyze the picture, in this case Figure 2.1, by using a series of questions:

- *Do the two data series appear to correlate well?* I answer this question simply by comparing the two data series and noting how well they seem to track one another. In Figure 2.1, they seem to correlate well; the data series move up and down at roughly the same time, with mortgage debt generally growing moderately faster than home prices.

- *Does it make common sense that the two data sets should correlate well?* In this case, yes, it does. The faster home prices go up, the more money homebuyers have to borrow in order to buy, and the more homeowners can borrow by taking out a home equity or second mortgage loan. So it is intuitively logical that home mortgage debt should change as home values do.

- *Do changes in one data set lead or precede the other?* In other words, does the movement of one variable seem to *cause* the movement of the other variable? To answer this question, I study the two data series, trying to see whether a change in one line appears to consistently precede a change in the other. I don't see a consistent pattern of causation in Figure 2.1. This means that one or more other economic factors drive both of them.

- *Does the correlation break down at times?* In Figure 2.1, I see three time periods where the correlation was weak. Twice—during the mid-to-late 1980s and the early 2000s—mortgage debt grew considerably faster than home prices. Then, more recently, home mortgage debt grew much more slowly than home prices. Correlation breakdowns are not a weakness of my method, but a strength, because they lead us to thinking about . . .

- *What other variables could be important?* Further testing that I don't present here shows that two other variables impact home mortgage debt growth. One is the loan-to-home-value (LTV) ratio, or how much people have already borrowed against the value of their homes. In 1952, the average LTV ratio in the US was a low 19%, so mortgage debt could safely grow faster than home prices for quite a while. That explains why mortgage debt could grow so quickly in the 1980s. By 1993, it was still only a perfectly wholesome 40%. The other important variable is home mortgage lending standards. During the early 2000s, lenders dramatically loosened up their standards, allowing more people to buy homes with weak credit histories and/or low down payments. The national LTV ultimately reached 64% in 2009. Since then, lenders have maintained very tight standards.

This kind of analysis limits the chances of my falling for some form of misleading economic reasoning. I stick with real data, and what the pictures of that real data teach me.

You might wonder why I don't choose to analyze the economy using statistics rather than pictures. Many economic experts work this way. Read any academic article from the social sciences, including the social science of economics, and you will invariably see scads of statistical analysis. For example, I pulled Figure 2.2 out of an article in a respected journal dedicated to the statistical study of economics.

Figure 2.2. An example of academic economists' statistical analysis. (Source: "Pareto tails in socio-economic phenomena: a kinetic description," by Stefano Gualandi and Giuseppe Toscani, *Economics*, May 18, 2018, page 6.)

The coefficients η_1, η_2 are random parameters, which are independent of v and w, and distributed so that always $v^*, w^* \geq 0$, i.e $\eta_1, \eta_2 \geq \gamma - 1$. Unless these random variables are centered, i.e $\langle \eta_1 \rangle = \langle \eta_2 \rangle = 0$, it is immediately seen that the mean wealth is not preserved, but it increases or decreases exponentially (see the computations in Cordier et al. (2005)). For centered η_i,

$$\langle v^* + w^* \rangle = (1 + \langle \eta_1 \rangle)v + (1 + \langle \eta_2 \rangle)w = v + w, \tag{9}$$

implying conservation of the average wealth. In this case, if the initial density $f_0(v)$, $v \in R_+$, satisfies the normalization conditions

$$\int_{R_+} f_0(v)\, dv = 1, \quad \int_{R_+} v f_0(v)\, dv = 1, \tag{10}$$

If you are thinking, "Yes, *that's* the kind of analysis I'm looking for!" put this book down and please never contact me. However, if you think that statistics can't be all bad, even amateurs like you and me can apply the basic correlation tool called *regression analysis*. It measures the degree of correlation between two sets of data by calculating a measurement called R^2. An R^2 of 100% reflects a perfect correlation, while an R^2 of 0% reflects no correlation at all. Microsoft's Excel software will calculate an R^2 for you in seconds. For example, it tells me that the R^2 between home mortgage debt and home prices between 1976 and 2016 was 60%.

But a chart tells you so much more than an R^2. It tells you *when* in time a correlation does or doesn't work, which helps you think through what other variables might be at play. And a chart allows you to identify whether one data set leads or lags the other data set, something an R^2 can't do. So, sorry, I will be using (almost) no statistics in this book. The only exceptions are a handful that make me look smart. Hey, it's my book.

Data Sources

I DON'T RELY ON SECRET DATA SOURCES THAT ONLY I, Julian Assange, and six teenage Russian hackers have access to. Rather, nearly all of my data comes from public sources, namely various government agencies. (I mentally allocate all of the federal taxes I pay to the selfless civil servants who collect, organize, and estimate the data I use.) My primary sources include:

- The Federal Reserve Bank of St. Louis, which maintains a massive online economic data base of other organizations' data it cutely calls FRED. FRED is a great first resource for locating any economic data, and is quite user friendly.

- The Board of Governors of the Federal Reserve System (the Fed), particularly its quarterly Financial Accounts of the United States, which is as awesome as it sounds.
- The Bureau of Economic Analysis (BEA), which is the source for gross domestic product (GDP) and personal income data.
- The Census Bureau (Census), which maintains a grab bag of population, housing, and other data, as well as the consumer price index (CPI) inflation rate.
- The Bureau of Labor Statistics (BLS), which bizarrely is the source for labor statistics, like jobs and unemployment.
- Yahoo Finance, which is my source for stock price histories and company earnings forecasts.
- Any book by P. G. Wodehouse, the creator of Jeeves and other unforgettable characters. P. G. offers no economic data whatsoever, but his novels provide amusing and refreshing respite from dense data tables.

I'll also give a shout-out to *The Wall Street Journal*, whose broad business, investment, and economics coverage often provides useful data. As a bonus, in its editorials and opinion columns, *The Wall Street Journal* also helps to spread a lot of the economic fables that I get to debunk in this book!

Data Limitations

AS MUCH AS I'D LIKE TO CLAIM that my charts are unimpeachable sources of scientific fact, I can't, for several reasons. The first is *a shortage of data history*. Let me explain.

Imagine that your doctor diagnosed you with a particular ailment and said, "Take this pill. The drug company tried it out on six people, and it seems to work." You would be appalled. *Six* people? If *600* people were tested, you might be interested. Make it *6,000*, and you'd be confident.

One of the fundamental tenets of statistical analysis is the importance of sample size. The experts say that, technically, you need at least 40 data points to have a 50% chance of predicting behavior, and at least 130 data points to have a 90% chance (Michael Lewis, *The Undoing Project*, page 161).

Unfortunately, sample sizes that big just don't exist in macroeconomics—especially considering that an economic "data point" is rarely a single figure, but rather the collection of figures that make up an economic cycle. Thus, the GDP figure reflecting economic growth for the third quarter of 1996 is not meaningful in itself; growth over the economic expansion of 1991-2000 is. Since that is the case, economists nearly always have far too few data points available to attain a high level of confidence in their conclusions. Even the longest available economic data series available cover little more than ten economic cycles. For example, the BEA's full set of GDP data only goes back to 1952. So it doesn't include a single economic depression.

The second problem is that the accuracy of the data always has to be questioned. Think about the monthly jobs report issued by the BLS. It comes out a few days after the end of the month. How the heck does the BLS accurately collect this data on a timely basis, with millions of US employers, the self-employed, new businesses creating jobs, failed businesses shedding jobs, and so many other phenomena to be tracked and analyzed?

The answer is that the data needs to be taken with a grain of salt. In fact, the BLS itself says that "the confidence interval for the monthly change in total nonfarm employment from the establishment survey is on the order of plus or minus 105,000." Considering that the average monthly growth reported by the BLS over the past two decades was 100,000, that's a wide "confidence interval." It means that the "real" job growth in a particular month when the average 100,000 figure was reported might have been anywhere from minus 5,000 to plus 205,000. True confidence in a job growth trend thus requires many months of BLS reports, along with other corroborating data like the direction of changes in unemployment claims or consumer spending.

Further, some of the data can seem plain wacky. One I've scratched my head about over time is the level of interest income Americans are supposedly earning, according to the monthly personal income report from the BEA. Anyone with a bank or money market account knows that, since 2008, the interest we earn on such accounts has been near zero. Figure 2.3 shows that, as expected, the interest on deposits *paid out* by a representative bank (Astoria Federal) plunged from 2007 until recently. But the picture also shows that, according to the BEA, interest income *received* over that time period by US households in total was pretty flat. What gives? Frankly, I have no idea.

Figure 2.3. Always question the data. For example, how have Astoria Bank's interest payments to depositors fallen sharply at the same time that the BEA's estimated interest received by households stayed flat? (Sources: National interest income—BEA. Astoria Bank deposit expense—company reports.)

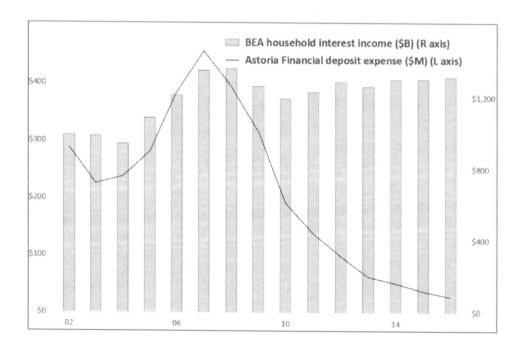

These caveats lead me to some important conclusions.

First, I humbly admit that even my brilliant pictures don't identify true, statistically significant "facts," but rather suggestive trends—broad patterns that can be useful in making wise financial decisions, including asset allocation choices.

Second, I try to find other relevant data that can confirm or refute the identified trend. For example, if Ford says that its car sales were up 10% last month, that doesn't mean all its peers in the auto industry must be doing the same. Maybe Ford had a sale. Maybe it increased its advertising. So if you're trying to understand national auto sales trends, check out GM's and Toyota's sales last month also.

Third, I continually think through whether the identified trend makes common sense. Is this how real human beings that I know actually behave? Have I seen this behavior in real life?

Fourth, recognizing that economic data analysis is a blunt instrument, I don't use my charts to make short-term investment decisions, like playing the stock market for a 5% move based on, say, the most recent GDP reading. Rather, I wait for clear and consistent evidence of *material* under- or over-valuation before adjusting my asset allocation, when I have a lot of confidence that taking action will eventually create a financial benefit.

3 My Asset Valuation Tool: The Earnings Yield Model

OKAY, SO DATA PRESENTED IN PICTURE FORM is my first tool for overcoming weaknesses in my economic thinking. What do I do with the data? I plug it into my second tool—an investment valuation model that logically links economic trends and asset prices to investment decisions.

Let me explain how the model is constructed, through an imaginary dialogue between Investor Eddie and employees from three fake companies:

- Banker Betty from the First National Bank of Hobbiton, the leading bank in Westfarthing.
- Nashid "Whiteshoes" Ng, Treasurer of Megalomania Industries, a conglomerate spanning industries from bird seed to ballistic missiles.
- Wheeler K. Deeler, chief financial officer of Internet midget Tweezer, which lets you send 16-character messages. (Helpfully, the service pops up with the standard format "__ sucks".)

The final character is Gary, your ne'er-do-well narrator, who will draw some real-world conclusions from the fake dialogue.

SETTING: An upscale bar in the Wall Street area. Investor Eddie, a successful barista and TV extra—he's played 136 dead guys on *Law and Order*—sits at a booth. Stage right, Banker Betty enters, turns off her cell phone for effect, and joins Eddie in the booth.

Scene 1: The Time Value of Money

INVESTOR EDDIE: I've saved $10,000 from tips. Where can I invest it to provide for my retirement?

BANKER BETTY: If you give my bank that $10,000 today, I promise to give you the whole $10,000 back in a year.

INVESTOR EDDIE: What? Give up my money for a year for nothing? I want a return on my investment if I give up the use of my money for a whole year.

BANKER BETTY: Okay, I'll give you a 1% interest rate for your patience. You'll get $10,100 in a year.

NARRATOR GARY: Any investment you make requires you to give up the use of your money for some period of time. Every dollar Eddie turns over to Betty could otherwise be used to support his lifestyle as an aspiring thespian. As an investor, you should always get paid for the time value of your money.

Scene 2: Current Inflation

INVESTOR EDDIE: Not so fast, banker lady. I just heard on the radio that prices are rising by 2% a year. So if you only give me $10,100 in a year, I'll be worse off than before! I won't even be able to buy then what I can today.

BANKER BETTY: Darn it, right you are. You want to earn the time value of your money *after* accounting for inflation. So my bank will pay you $10,300 after a year. That makes a 3% interest rate. And I'll throw in a free *Lord of the Rings* calendar.

NARRATOR GARY: Now Banker Betty has edged her way into the real world. The investment she describes is a cash investment like the one I discussed earlier—namely, a 1-year bank certificate of deposit (CD) or a 1-

year Treasury bill. Both offer a 1-year fixed payment that should compensate investors for current inflation plus time value. Both are guaranteed by the federal government—the Treasury bill directly, and the bank CD through the Federal Deposit Insurance Corporation (FDIC), which is in turn is backed by the government up to $250,000 per depositor per bank. So while the offered 3% return is low, the tradeoff is that your money is safe, and that it will not lose purchasing power based on the current inflation rate.

Scene 3: Future Inflation Risk, Plus the Long-Term Value of Money

BANKER BETTY: If you like that deal, I've got an even better one for you. Instead of just a 1-year loan, my bank will pay you 3% a year for five years!

INVESTOR EDDIE: Are you crazy? Now you're trying to cheat me in two ways, lady. First, you're asking me to tie up my money for five years, not just one year. Second, what if inflation rises higher than 2% during the next five years? I need to get paid for both of these risks. I want a 5% interest rate for five years, not 3%.

BANKER BETTY: Well played, Eddie, well played! You're right—you deserve more for the longer tie-up and for taking that extra inflation risk.

NARRATOR GARY: The real-world example of an investment along these lines is a Treasury bond, which comes in terms ranging from two to 30 years. Again the principal and interest are guaranteed by Uncle Sam, but here the investor bears the risk that inflation rises during the term of the bond and eats away at the real return. Therefore, a 10-year Treasury bond nearly always pays a higher interest rate than a 1-year Treasury bill.

Scene 4: Default Risk

BANKER BETTY EXITS LEFT, eager to make her pilates class. Nashid "White-shoes" Ng enters right, accompanied by three sniveling assistant vice presidents. (In the theater, assistant VPs never get to hold their heads high.)

WHITESHOES NG: Eddie, Megalomania Industries needs money to finance our new Bazookas by Beiber product line. We're looking to borrow from some smart individual investors like you. I'll match that 5% a year for five years that a bank will pay you.

INVESTOR EDDIE: No go, Ng. I need more than 5% a year from you. I know Megalomania has paid its bills for a long time. But unlike my bank account, my loan to you won't be backed by Uncle Sam. If Megalomania gets in trouble for selling bazookas to minors, you may have trouble paying me. I want 7% from you to make it worth my while to take the risk.

WHITESHOES (admiringly): You drive a hard bargain, Eddie. The 7% interest rate is yours.

NARRATOR GARY: Megalomania Industries is fictitious, but this investment type is not. An example is an investment-grade corporate bond, issued by a stable company with strong cash flow relative to its debt level. This means that the risk that the company won't be able to pay back the loan—the *default risk*—is relatively low. A bond of this kind generally has a maturity of ten years or longer. Examples of investment-grade companies are Apple and Exxon. As you will see, default risk is one of several forms of *market risk*.

Scene 5: Other Forms of Market Risk

WHITESHOES NG EXITS LEFT along with the three assistant VPs, who continue to snivel to beat the band. Wheeler K. Deeler enters right.

WHEELER K. DEELER: Eddie, Tweezer needs money to buy a foosball table—my unpaid 23-year-old interns are getting restless. And our only cash flow is coming from ads for adult entertainment web sites working out of Honduras. So, like Megalomania, we're also in the market for a loan. Eddie, I'll pay you the same 7% a year that Megalomania offered. And I'll throw in fake news attacks on five of your frenemies.

INVESTOR EDDIE: Nice try, Deeler, but no dice. The world of high-tech startups is notoriously risky. You guys could go belly-up any day, and my only collateral will be a used foosball table. And even if you don't go bust, who could I get to buy me out if I need money fast? I want 10% a year if I'm going to lend my hard-earned tip money to your flimsy outfit.

WHEELER K. DEELER: Not cool, Eddie. No can do.

NARRATOR GARY: An example of this kind of investment: a *high-yield corporate bond*. This is a bond issued by a company with a weak cash flow and/or lots of debt. High-yield bonds are less politely called *junk bonds*. The default risk involved in buying a junk bond is much higher than on an investment-grade bond. And it can be harder to find a buyer for a junk bond when you want to sell. In fact, a high-yield bond investor takes on risks that are normally borne only by stock investors. The tradeoff for taking on these extra risks is that you receive a higher, and sometimes much higher, interest rate than you would on an investment grade bond.

Scene 6: Earnings Growth

WHEELER K. DEELER: Okay, how about this, Eddie? For ten thousand bucks, you can have 1% ownership of the company. Things are happening here at Tweezer. We're talking with a bunch of new advertisers now. World Federated Wrestling, Jim Beam, Smith & Wesson—they all fit our demographic. We could be big. And when that foosball table shows up, employee morale will soar. Get in on the ground floor, Eddie!

INVESTOR EDDIE: Sounds intriguing, Deeler. I know that insulting strangers is a growth business. I'm in.

NARRATOR GARY: An example of this kind of investment: *common stock*, which gives you part ownership of a public company. For example, buying one share of McDonald's stock gives you 0.00000012% ownership of the company. And free ketchup with every purchase of French fries.

THE CURTAIN FALLS. Wild applause, interrupted by a high-pitched scream.

The Earnings Yield Formula

SO MUCH FOR MY LITTLE DRAMA. Very little, I hear you saying. The purpose of my playlet is to introduce you to the key elements that impact the value of any investment. To review, they are:

The time value of money (T), or the amount you earn for tying up your money in an investment for some period of time.

Inflation (I) over the period of your investment. It could be the current actual inflation rate for a short-term investment like a 1-year CD, or expected long-term inflation for a 10-year Treasury bond.

Market risk (R), which includes the default risk I discussed in the drama, plus other risks that I'll detail in chapter four.

Earnings growth (G).

Using these variables, we can calculate the earnings yield model components for our three different core investments: a 1-year CD, a 10-year Treasury bond, and the S&P 500 index., as follows.

I'll start with a 1-year CD (CD). To be fairly priced, its yield should equal:

The short-term ($_{ST}$) time value of money (T) + the current ($_{C}$) inflation rate (I), or

$$CD = T_{ST} + I_C$$

The fair return on a 10-year Treasury bond (B) should equal:

The long-term (LT) time value of money + expected (E) future inflation, or

$$B = T_{LT} + I_E$$

Finally, the return on a stock investment is the earnings per share (E) of the business divided by the stock price (P). E/P should equal:

The 10-year Treasury bond yield (B) + market risk (R) – earnings growth (G), or

$$E/P = B + R - G$$

When an *actual* calculated return varies noticeably from its *expected* fair value, an investment extreme is present that we investors can take advantage of.

Now that we've identified the investment variables, let's put some numbers to them and begin to explore the factors that drive them in real life. That's the focus of the next two chapters.

4 Drivers of the Cash and Bond Earnings Yields: The Time Value of Money and Inflation

IN CHAPTER THREE, I created formulas for valuing cash (1-year CD) and bond (10-year Treasury) investments. The cash formula is:

The short-term (ST) time value of money + the current (C) inflation rate, or

$$CD = T_{ST} + I_C$$

The bond formula is:

The long-term (LT) time value of money + expected (E) future inflation, or

$$B = T_{LT} + I_E$$

To estimate the fair values for cash and bonds, we need to estimate the time value of money and inflation. Sleeves rolled up? Good. Let's get to it.

The Time Value of Money

IN THE LITTLE DRAMA FEATURED IN CHAPTER THREE, I said that we investors get paid a "real return" above the inflation rate on our investments in exchange for giving up control of our money during the investment period. Logically, the time value of money should be a pretty stable figure. But it's not, and the reason lies in what actually drives cash and bond investment yields.

To explain how the system works, let's start with a history of the "real yield" on the 1-year CD. The real yield is the stated, or nominal, yield on the 1-year bank CD less the current inflation rate, which is a way to calculate the time value of money. I use the consumer price index (CPI) as the inflation rate measure. The history of the real yield is shown in Figure 4.1.

Figure 4.1. A history of the short-term time value of money. Over the period shown, the value averaged 1.5%. (Sources: 1-year CD yield—Fed, Federal Deposit Insurance Corporation. Inflation—BLS.)

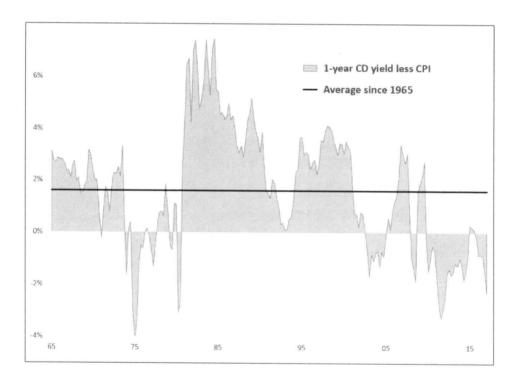

The historical average real yield of about 1.5% (indicated by the horizontal line in the graph) makes sense. But why the huge variation, shown by the wild up-and-down gyrations of the quarterly bars? And why has the real cash yield been largely *negative* since 2009? Why would investors *pay* someone to hold their cash?

The answer is that investors are actually not the ones who set the real cash yield. The Federal Reserve does this by adjusting its fed funds rate. The fed funds rate is the interest rate on money that one bank lends to another. Set by the Federal Reserve, it's a major determinant of the interest rate that banks will pay to consumers and businesses. It's also one of the main levers that the Fed uses to try to influence the US economy. (By the way, it fails in the attempt, as I'll discuss in chapter seven.)

Figure 4.2 compares the historic rates on the 1-year bank CD and the Federal Reserve's fed funds rate. They have been nearly identical.

Figure 4.2. The Federal Reserve largely sets the 1-year bank CD rate, which means that it also sets the short-term time value of money. (Sources: 1-year CD—Fed, Federal Deposit Insurance Corporation. Fed funds rate—Fed.)

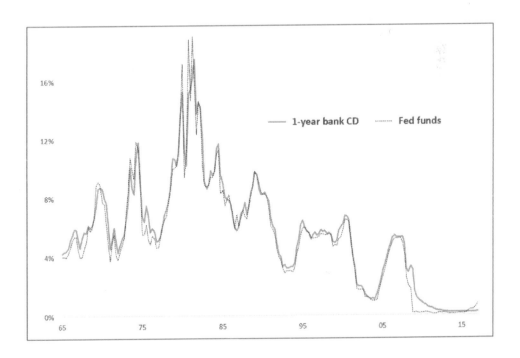

Notice how closely changes in the fed funds rate track the changes in the cash yield. Investors don't *demand* a certain investment return from borrowers; they are *given* a return by the Federal Reserve. Or not given it, as is the case today. You may find this knowledge a bit of a blow to your self-esteem—I certainly do. But there it is: The Federal Reserve bosses you and me around. Those patrician bullies.

Let's move on to the time value of money for longer-term bond investments.

Figure 4.3. The Federal Reserve is also the key driver of bond interest rates. (Source: Fed.)

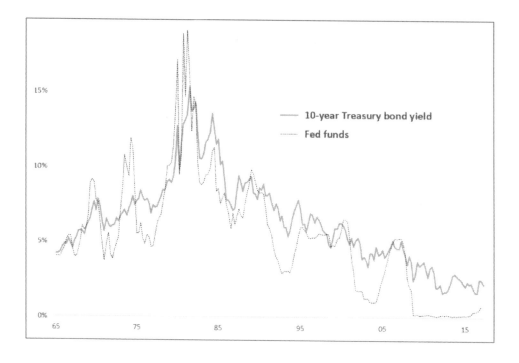

To calculate the time value of money for this longer-term investment, I compare the 10-year Treasury bond yield to economists' expected average inflation rate over the next ten years, as shown in Figure 4.3. Note that the graph starts in 1990, because that is when the economists' survey began. It therefore doesn't include the high-time-value periods of the 1970s and 1980s. To compensate, I rounded up the 1990-forward average rate from 1.9% to my long-term estimate of 2.5%.

Figure 4.4. A history of the long-term time value of money, which is the 10-year Treasury bond yield less the expected long-term inflation rate. I rounded up to arrive at the 2.5% long-term average. (Sources: Interest rates—Fed. Inflation—BLS.)

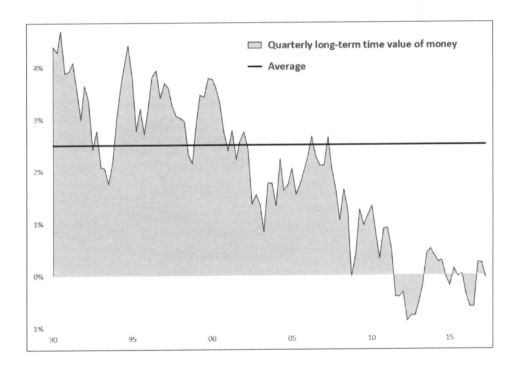

The story of the time value of money component of a US Treasury bond investment is similar to that of the 1-year CD. First, the Federal Reserve is clearly a major driver of the 10-year Treasury bond yield, as Figure 4.3 shows. The relationship is not quite as close as with the 1-year CD, where regression analysis reveals that fed funds changes explain 97% of 1-year CD rate changes. But it's close, with a very high 81% correlation between the two rates. See how I slipped in some statistics that make me look smart?

In sum, I have set the "normal" time value of money as 1.5% for the 1-year CD and 2.5% for the 10-year Treasury bond. Recognize that these are judgment calls, not precise scientific calculations, because our data sets are limited (starting in 1964 for the one-year CD and in 1990 for the 10-year Treasury), and because some unusual things happened during those periods (soaring inflation, two debt bubbles, and wild swings in Federal Reserve policy). But both estimates make rough common sense.

The most important investment conclusion: It is very clear that the actual time value of money earned by both CD and bond investors is largely driven by the Federal Reserve.

Now let's move on to the next variable in the earnings yield formula: inflation.

Inflation

INFLATION HAS A HUGE IMPACT ON INVESTMENT RETURNS. For example, look at the pain that was inflicted on the stock market by the Great Inflation—the inflation bubble of the 1970 and early 1980s (Figure 4.5).

Figure 4.5. Inflation restrained stock prices for over a decade. When inflation ebbed, stock prices soared. (Sources: S&P 500 Index—Yahoo Finance. CPI—BLS.)

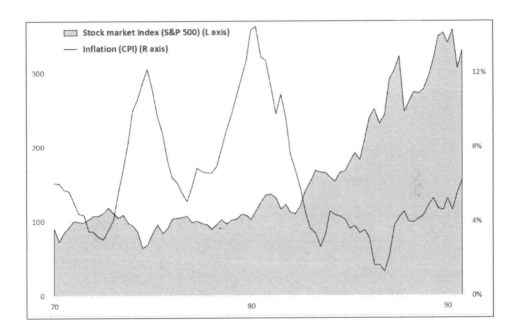

In fact, as I mentioned in chapter three, the best investment of the 1970s was cash: During that decade, you would have done best by leaving your money in the bank!

It would have been nice to be able to figure out in advance that inflation was going to be a problem for stocks and bonds during the late 1970s and early 1980s, and that slowing inflation would create tremendous investment opportunities over the following three decades. It's a good example of why being able to make accurate economic forecasts can be tremendously valuable to the investor. So let's investigate what the key drivers of inflation are.

Figure 4.6 shows a long-term history of US inflation, going back to the 1870s. It is based on research by economist Robert Shiller.

Figure 4.6. This long-term history of the US inflation rate shows major swings. Why? (Source: Robert Shiller, from Measuringworth.com.)

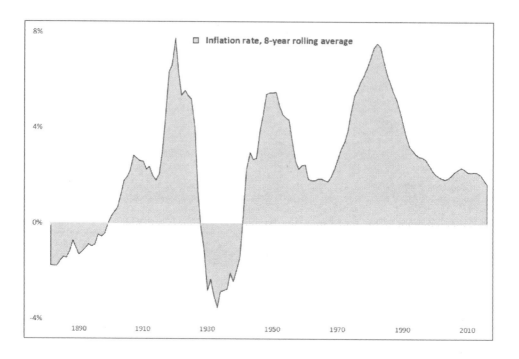

As you can see, there have been some pretty big swings in the inflation rate over time, including:

- Deflation during the late nineteenth century and during the Great Depression of the 1930s.
- Sharp inflation spikes following World War I (during the 1920s) and World War II (during the 1950s).
- The Great Inflation of the 1970s and early 1980s, set off by the "guns and butter" government policies of supporting both the Vietnam War and the Great Society poverty programs.
- The Great Moderation in inflation over the past three decades.

To explain inflation's volatility, I'll apply one of the best-known classical economics concepts, and one that even actually works a lot in practice—supply and demand. According to that theory, inflation rises in response to one of three kinds of changes in supply and demand: an increase in demand for a good or service; a decrease in the supply of a good or service; or an increase in the supply of money. I'll explain each of these three possibilities with another corny story.

Demand for a good or service rises. Assume my grocery store, Gary's Eats, buys 40 lemons a day to meet the typical demand for that fruit, selling them for 50¢ apiece. All of a sudden, a craze for gin fizzes arises. A properly made gin fizz, as I don't have to remind you, requires three quarters of an ounce of lemon juice. Lemon demand rises to 60 a day. But I still can buy only 40 lemons a day because that's all the lemon growers are producing. I take advantage of the heightened demand by raising the price of a lemon to 70¢, which slows demand back to 40 a day. So, an example of price inflation caused by increased demand.

Supply of a good or service falls. The gin fizz craze dies; lychee martinis are all the rage now. Lemon demand is back to 40 a day, and my price is back to 50¢. But the greasy spot fungus (a real thing, look it up) is doing a number on citrus trees. Growers have to ration their scant supplies of lemons, so Gary's Eats now only gets 20 a day. I raise my lemon price back to 70¢ to reduce demand to 20. Voila: an example of price inflation due to decreased supply.

The supply of money rises. Lemon growers attack the greasy fungus using a copper fungicide (obviously!), and my lemon supply returns to its original 40 a day, and the price to 50¢. But then local Internet company Tweezer is bought by Twister, a Chinese Internet behemoth. All of the Tweezer employees in the neighborhood get big bonuses and start throwing their newfound money around. I'm no dummy. I change the name of my grocery to Gary's Hole Foods, make the male staff wear man buns, and raise lemon prices to 70¢ apiece to get my share of the newly expanded local money supply. Q.E.D. An example of price inflation due to an increased money supply.

Those are the theoretical possibilities. But I'm not about theory. So let's consider some of the economic variables that might appear to drive national inflation in real life, and see whether the data supports what classical economics suggests.

Is Inflation Driven by Total Demand?

ECONOMIC DEMAND ON A NATIONAL SCALE is measured as real GDP, which is the dollar value of all the goods and services that are purchased in the country during a particular time period. The word "real" in this case means that changes in inflation are theoretically taken out, so the remaining real GDP counts only units of goods and services purchased. By contrast, "nominal" GDP measures the dollar value of production using actual prices that are impacted by inflation. For example, according to the bean counters over at the BEA, in the first quarter of 2016, nominal GDP grew by 2.8% from the year before. However, inflation was estimated to be 1.2% during that year, so real GDP grew by 1.6%. In other words, Americans bought 1.6% more units of goods and services in the first quarter of 2016 than the prior year, and paid 1.2% more for each unit purchased.

Real GDP, then, is a more meaningful measure of demand than nominal GDP, and we'll use it for that purpose. Our question: Is there a real-world connection between US aggregate unit demand, as measured by real GDP, and inflation? Figure 4.7 shows the data.

Figure 4.7. Has changing demand for goods and services (defined as real GDP) driven inflation? Surprisingly, no. (Sources: Real GDP—BEA. Inflation rate—BLS.)

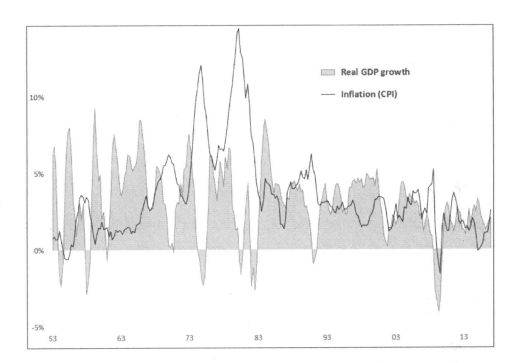

The picture simply does not show a correlation. Many times, total demand (as measured by GDP) grew strongly while inflation fell, and vice versa. Total demand is off the list of possible US inflation drivers.

Is Inflation Driven by Commodity Prices?

COULD RISING COMMODITY COSTS drive inflation? In general, the answer is no. Tangible goods make up only about one third of the US economy; various services make up the rest. And even when we buy tangible goods, their commodity cost component is not that large. For example, the lumber, pipes, wires, and other stuff that goes into a house only make up about one quarter of the total construction cost. Labor is a bigger cost. So commodities, in general, are not important enough as a price factor to impact overall inflation.

But one commodity is an exception to the rule. You guessed it—oil. The magical fluid that runs our cars, heats our homes, and lubricates our baseball mitts. Actually, forget that last part—baseball gloves are softened with neatsfoot oil, which is made from the shin bones and feet of cattle. That nugget alone is worth the price of this book.

Oil and other energy sources are a significant driver of our economy. We spend about 7% of our incomes on energy, and even with the growing importance of sustainable energy sources such as wind and solar power, the majority of energy spending is for oil and related products, like natural gas. So when the Organization of the Petroleum Exporting Countries (OPEC, the cartel of oil-producing nations), decided to reduce the supply of oil to the West in the 1970s, the resulting price spike materially impacted overall inflation, as Figure 4.8 shows.

Figure 4.8. Oil price changes explain a significant portion of the changes in inflation from 1970 to 1990. (Sources: Inflation rate—BLS. Oil prices—Federal Reserve Bank of St. Louis.)

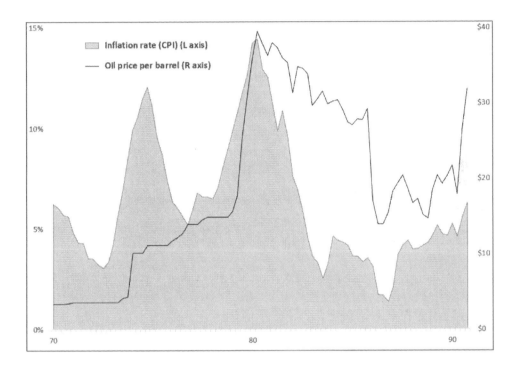

Subsequent to 1990, inflation and oil prices were only loosely correlated, because of greater energy efficiency, conservation efforts, and increased supply. But then came the shale revolution, as Figure 4.9 shows.

Figure 4.9. Oil prices continue to have an impact on inflation, albeit muted in comparison to the 1970-1990 period. (Sources: Inflation rate—BLS. Oil prices—Federal Reserve Bank of St. Louis.)

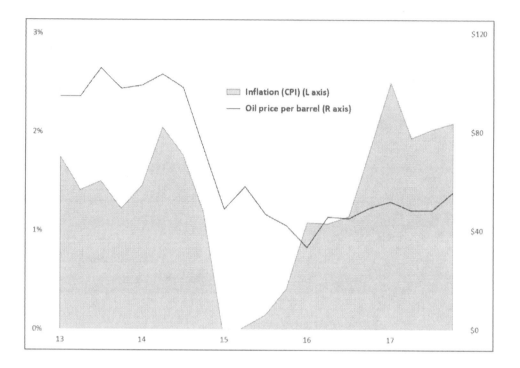

In sum, the price of oil is a material driver of inflation.

Is Inflation Driven by Trade?

RECALL FROM FIGURE 4.6 that there were three long periods during which inflation fell drastically. The most dramatic was the major deflation (that is, a period of overall price declines) during the 1930s, concurrent with the Great Depression. That deflation was caused by a major collapse in demand; real GDP fell by an unprecedented 26% from 1929 to 1933. But the other two periods of falling inflation—the deflation that occurred during the late nineteenth century and the sharp decline in inflation during the Great Moderation of the late 1980s and the 1990s—coincided with healthy economic growth.

What caused these two periods of deflation combined with increased demand? I argue that it was in large part due to sharply increased trade. Two charts support this argument.

First, consider Figure 4.10, which shows how railroad transport exploded in the latter half of the nineteenth century.

Figure 4.10. The rapid expansion of US railroads in the latter half of the nineteenth century supported increased trade, which in turn drove inflation lower. (Source: Association of American Railroads.)

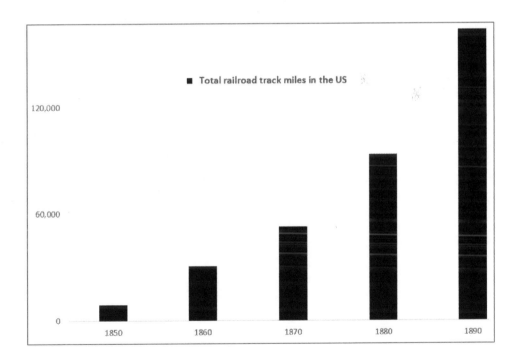

Build-out of the railroad system in the late nineteenth century led to a US trade boom—with other countries, yes, but, more important, with ourselves. Prior to then, goods were hard to move. Imagine hauling a wagonload of corn from Iowa to Boston in 1850. No fun, I'd bet. And when you reached your destination after three months of traveling over potholed roads, the corn might not have been as fresh as discerning Bostonians would have liked. The advent of the railroads made goods transport far easier—and cheaper. Think of all those farm goods pouring eastward from the fertile Midwest and all of those Northeast manufactured goods heading westward at a fraction of prior shipping costs. The reduction in transport cost was a powerful force for lower price inflation, as well as better productivity, in the nineteenth century. (Not the only force, mind you—an immigration wave and the restraining force of the gold standard also restrained inflation.)

Now for the Great Moderation in inflation since the early 1980s. Figure 4.11, on the next page, shows that imports from abroad became a powerful force for price deflation in the late twentieth century.

A careful look at Figure 4.11 appears to show a decidedly mixed influence of trade on inflation. Imports and inflation *both* grew from 1965 to 1980. Only after that date do we see the deflationary impact that I attribute to imports.

What's the explanation? The following two facts. First, in the 1960s, imports, while rising, were still too small in volume to materially influence overall inflation. Second, in the 1970s, the major US import was oil, which as I said above soared in price and pushed up inflation. Only when oil prices sta-bilized in the 1980s did cheaper goods imports begin to make their mark as a deflationary force.

Figure 4.11. Sharp growth in low-priced imports helped restrain inflation in the late 20th century. (Sources: Goods imports and consumption—BEA. Inflation—BLS.)

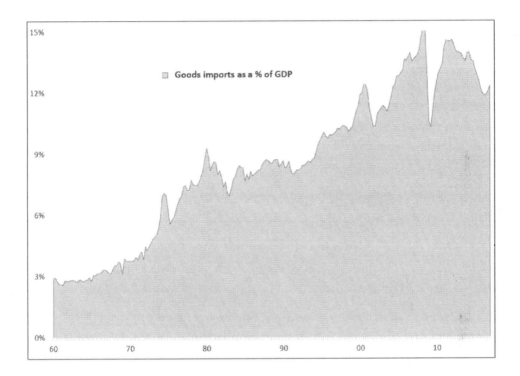

And Figure 4-12 illustrates that rising imports still help to moderate US inflation growth.

Figure 4.12. Import prices have consistently risen more slowly than domestic prices, restraining inflation. The available data goes back 15 years. (Sources: CPI index—BLS. Import price index—BEA.)

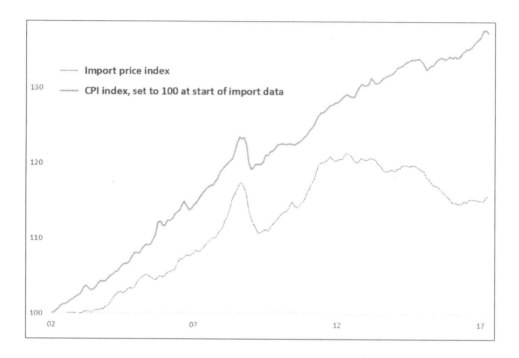

Some imports to the US are products that aren't or can't be made here, like Moët champagne or authentic Gouda cheese. But most imports are similar to American-made products, only cheaper. For example, TV sets assembled in China or garments produced in Bangladesh. Back in the 1960s, imports were only 2% of GDP, so they didn't serve as a material price check on American goods. But by 2000, imports surpassed 12% of GDP.

The conclusion: Import volume has a material impact on overall inflation. When imports are a large and growing economic presence, they tend to restrain price increases.

Is Inflation Driven by the Cost of Labor?

IN RECENT YEARS, NATIONAL POLITICS HAS FEATURED a lot of debate about the struggles of middle-class and working-class people. There's a general perception that wages have stagnated over the past few decades. Is this correct? And if so, could this trend be related to the low rate of price inflation we've observed since the 1990s?

First, it is true that the growth rate of wages per job steadily fell since 1980. Figure 4.13 tells the story.

Figure 4.13. The trend of wage growth per job has steadily declined since 1980. (Sources: Wages—BEA. Jobs—BLS.)

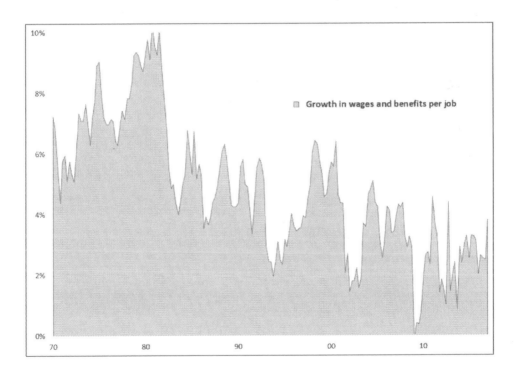

Why the slowing wage growth? Classical economics says the reason could be an increase in the supply of people looking for a job. But in fact the opposite has happened, as Figure 4.14 shows.

Figure 4.14. Has an increase in the growth rate of supply of US labor been the cause of slowing wage growth? Not at all. (Sources: Labor force—BLS. Population—BEA.)

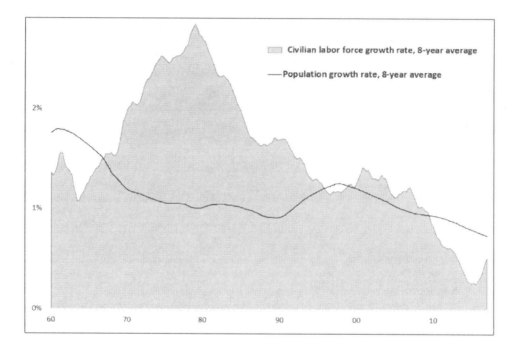

The figure shows that, since about 1980, the number of people counted in the labor pool has been growing slowly—and since about the year 2010 even slower than population growth. Slowing growth in the number of job seekers should theoretically *increase* wage rates. The cause of declining wage growth therefore has to be found on the demand side for labor rather than the supply side.

One labor demand squeeze we just discussed—trade. The *US trade balance* measures the relationship between imports and exports. Trade's connection with the overall health of the economy is complex (no, I'm not getting sucked into a tariff discussion), but in general it is clear that when imports are much greater than exports, US workers take a hit, because foreign workers are replacing US workers, which reduces the demand for US labor. The US trade balance has in fact shifted significantly—from a positive balance of +1% of GDP in the 1960s to a deficit as great as -6%. Recently, the trade deficit has been about -3%. This change in the trade balance has reduced the demand for US labor and therefore exerted a downward pressure on wages.

Another deflationary influence on wages is technology. By replacing people with machines (or today with computer algorithms), technology reduces the demand for labor, leading to lower wages. Thirty years ago, my commute to my office desk would include a stop at a gas station to have the attendant fill my tank, a nod to the elevator operator in my building, and a hello to my secretary before I entered my office. Today, barely any of those jobs exists. One day, I won't even be driving my car—and my office job may not exist. It's all basic and inevitable economics, however painful.

The declining demand for labor has led to a decline in the negotiating power of US workers. That decreased negotiating power is reflected in falling rates of union membership. In 1983, 17% of private sector workers in the US were union members. That percentage is down to 7% today. Whatever your view of unions, we can all agree that their shrinking presence indicates less demand for US workers and downward pressure on wages.

My conclusion: The balance between the supply and demand for labor is a driver of inflation. Over the past three decades, falling labor demand has outpaced slowing supply, thereby depressing wages and contributing to lower rates of inflation.

Is Inflation Driven by the Money Supply?

AT THE START OF THIS CHAPTER, I noted the theory that an increase in the supply of money, all else equal, drives up prices and causes inflation. To test this idea in the real world, we have to answer four questions:

- What do we mean by "money"?
- Where does money come from?
- How should the supply of money theoretically link to inflation?
- Does that theoretical link actually exist in the real world?

What do we mean by "money"? This seems like a dumb question. Money is green paper with a dead president on it. But the reality is a bit more complicated. It turns out that economists recognize five different definitions of money, cleverly named M1 through M5. We need to choose one. I'll pick M2, the most common definition of money. It includes cash, checking accounts, savings accounts, money market accounts, and CDs. That's largely the same as my investment category of cash.

Where does money come from? Do storks have two jobs? Do automatic teller machines make money? Does Warren Buffett print it in his basement? All good guesses. But in fact, those folks at the Federal Reserve are the core money makers in the US. I won't go into the gory details, but by trading with banks they can grow or shrink the supply of money in the US.

How should the supply of money theoretically link to inflation? Through the classic economic formula to which I referred in chapter one:

$$MV = PY$$

In the formula, M is the supply of money, P is prices of goods and services, and Y is the number of units of goods and services we buy (equivalent to real GDP). These three variables are connected by V, or velocity. Think of velocity as the speed at which money is recycled through the economy. The recycling is done by the banking system. When the Fed creates money, it doesn't go directly to us, but rather to banks. In order to get the money to us, the banks have to lend it to us. The rate at which they do this is the V in the money supply formula.

One historically popular theory about the "MV = PY" relationship is called *monetarism*. Monetarism assumes that velocity (V) is a constant, and that real unit GDP (Y) is relatively unaffected by changes in the money supply. If V and Y can't significantly change, the only other variable that can shift in response to changes in the money supply (M) is price (P). Monetarists therefore believe that changes in the money supply largely drive prices, and that increases in the money supply that are faster than real GDP growth therefore creates inflation.

Creating a super-simple economy will illustrate the monetarist theory. This economy consists solely of 100 annual kiwi sales, bought by customers 25 at a time every three months. The Kiwi National Bank holds $100 of the customers' money, which they use four times a year to buy kiwis. Plugging these variables into the money supply formula, we get $100 (M) x 4 (V) = P x 100. Solving for P, the price the customers can pay, gives $4 per kiwi. If the Kiwi National Bank prints another $50 of money, the equation is $150 x 4 = P x 100. Now the customers will pay $6 for each kiwi because the supply of money has increased. Voila—inflation! That's the theory. But what are the facts?

Does monetarism's theory about the tight link between the money supply and inflation work in the real world? See for yourself (Figure 4.15).

Figure 4.15. Does the growth rate of the money supply (M2) drive inflation? Not at all. (Sources: Money supply—Fed. Inflation rate—BLS.)

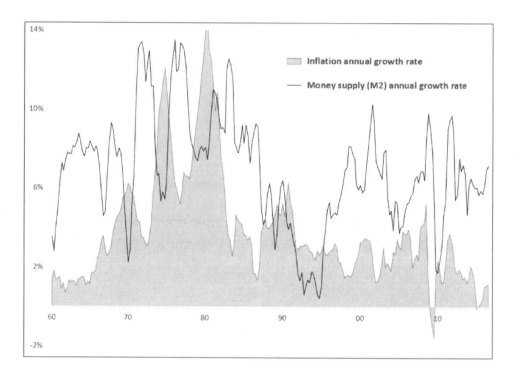

The chart shows that in fact there is no clear link between money supply growth and inflation. For example, money supply growth in recent years was nearly as fast as it was during the Great Inflation of the 1970s. Yet inflation today is dramatically lower than it was then.

The problem with the monetarist theory turns out to be the assumption that velocity is stable. In fact, it isn't, as Figure 4.16 shows.

Figure 4.16. The velocity of money is not stable. Banks lend out money (M2) at differing speeds over time. (Sources: Money supply—Fed. GDP—BEA.)

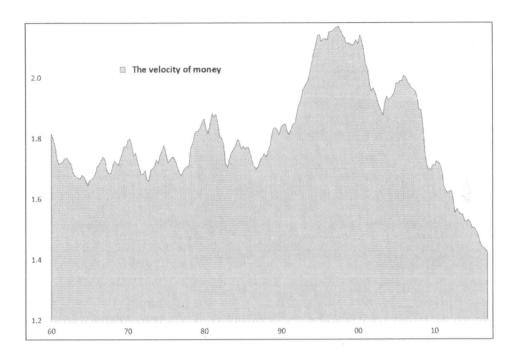

If you were a monetarist in 1990, you were pretty smug: Velocity had been stable for three decades. But since then, your smug little world got rocked. Velocity soared during the 1990s, then went into a nearly two-decades-long tail spin. What happened?

One destabilizer of velocity was the creation of *asset-backed securities* (ABS). ABS are an investment vehicle that basically take the banks out of their traditional role as middlemen between savers and borrowers. They allow consumers and businesses to borrow directly from investors. That in turn allows lending—and demand, as measured by GDP—to delink somewhat from the money supply. So a rise in ABS should show up as a rise in velocity, and vice versa. And in fact that is what happened, as Figure 4.17 shows.

Figure 4.17. The velocity of money has been greatly influenced by the advent of asset-based securities (ABS). (Sources: GDP—BEA. Money supply and ABS outstanding—Fed.)

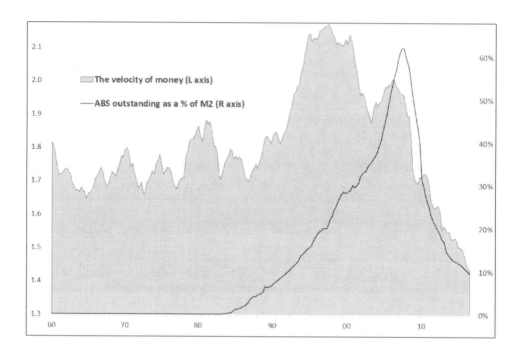

In practice, ABS were used largely to finance riskier loans, especially riskier home mortgages. Lenders loved ABS: They earned fees for arranging the loans, but transferred the risk of holding the loans from themselves to other investors. During the peak of the housing bubble, the volume of outstanding subprime and other risky home-mortgage loans held in ABS rose from $669 billion (end of 2003) to a whopping $2.3 trillion (mid-2007). Since then, massive defaults of those securities unsurprisingly discouraged investors, there has been essentially no new issuance of home mortgage ABS. So outstanding home-mortgage ABS fell to about $500 billion. That pattern of sharp upswing followed by dramatic collapse explains a lot about the changes in velocity over that period.

In conclusion, changes in the money supply are *not* a significant driver of inflation. But the velocity at which banks and other lenders circulate the money supply *is*. So lender willingness to lend is another important driver of inflation.

ॐ

TO RECAP, the drivers of inflation that I have identified are:

- Lender willingness to lend
- The demand for labor
- The trade balance
- The price of oil

In the next chapter, we'll examine the possible drivers of the earnings yield formula for the third major category of investment—stocks.

5 Drivers of the Stock Earnings Yield: Market Risk and Earnings Growth

IN CHAPTER THREE, I explained that the return on a stock investment is the earnings per share (E) of a business divided by its stock price (P). This earnings yield in turn should equal:

The 10-year Treasury bond yield (B) + market risk (R) – earnings growth (G), or

$$E/P = B + R - G$$

I explained the 10-year Trasury bond drivers (inflation and the time value of money) in the last chapter. Now it's time to identify drivers of the two other major components of the earnings yield model—market risk and earnings growth. I'll start with market risk.

In chapter two, I noted that one form of market risk is the possibility of bond default. Default risk is greater for high-yield bonds than for investment-grade bonds, and more costly for owners of stocks than bonds. When a company goes bust, bondholders may lose 20 to 40% of their principal invested, but stockholders lose all or nearly all.

While the possibility of default is the most important market risk, it is not the only one. Two other important ones are *earnings volatility risk* and *liquidity risk*.

Earnings volatility risk. A fall in company earnings reduces the likelihood that a business can keep paying the interest on its bonds, and reduces the value of owning a share of the business. For example, the earnings of Macy's, like those of other brick-and-mortar department stores, have been hurt by online retailers like Amazon. Its expected earnings per share (EPS) is $3.83 for 2018, and Wall Street analysts expect a further decline to $3.49 next year, which is 21% below its 2013 EPS. As a result, a Macy's bond due in 2043 declined in value to 78 as of May, 2017, while the stock dropped by half over the past three years.

But the value of an investment can also be reduced just by earnings volatility, which means wide swings in earnings, or even just the fear that such swings could occur. We humans typically favor stability and try to avoid volatility. For example, both Clorox and Ford Motor make mature products—laundry bleach and cars. The annual sales growth of both companies averaged 2% per year for the five years from 2011 to 2016. Yet as of mid-2018, Clorox's stock price sold at 23 times its expected 2018 earnings, while Ford's stock sold at only seven times. That's because bleach is a steady seller, while car sales go through volatile cycles due to economic, technological and even commodity price (oil) changes. (Hey, "oil changes." Get it?) The greater volatility of Ford's earnings means greater perceived risk.

Liquidity risk. No, investing does not increase the danger of excessive dampness. For investors, liquidity is the ease of buying or selling a security at a stable price. When an investment is hard to buy or sell, its value suffers. For example, in 2008, in the midst of the Great Recession, the junk bond yield hit 20%. Few expected loss rates on junk bonds to rise high enough to justify that yield. Rather, the yield got so high because many investors in late 2008 were desperate to sell their junk investments, while very few brave souls were willing to step up and buy them. As a result of this illiquidity, the price of the bonds plummeted, causing their yield to skyrocket.

One way to measure liquidity is to look at the spread between the bid price—what potential buyers offer to pay for a security—and the ask price, which is what current owners of the security are willing to sell it for. A recent bid/asked quote for Apple stock was 174.36/174.37. The tiny bid/ask spread of $0.01 reflects an investment that is very liquid. On the other hand, small company Educational Development Corporation had a bid/ask spread of 12.90/13.00—a much wider $0.10. And on the same day, another small company, Monarch Cement, hadn't traded a single share—a real liquidity challenge.

Market Risk Measures: *Vive La Similitude*

MARKET RISK is a continually-changing investment variable. Tough economic times ratchet up perceived market risk, while periods of steady growth dial that perception down. As an investor, you'd like a tool that enables you to easily and accurately quantify the current level of perceived market risk. We could then plug that perceived risk level into the earnings yield formula, helping us arrive at an accurate calculation of the real value of our stock investments.

Is there such a tool? It turns out that there are *several* such tools. Here are three:

- *The investment-grade corporate bond spread to Treasuries,* which compares the yield on an average 10-year investment-grade corporate bond to the yield on a 10-year Treasury bond. For example, an IBM bond due in 2025 yielded 3.7% during May 2018, while the 7-year Treasury yielded 2.9%, for a 0.8% spread.

- *The high-yield corporate bond spread to Treasuries.* Same idea as above, just substituting a riskier bond for the investment-grade bond. Again, the higher the spread, the greater the perceived business risk. For example, junk-bond rated Tesla's bond due in 2025 yielded 7.6% during May 2018, a 4.9% spread over the comparable maturity Treasury bond.

- *The VIX.* This is the ticker symbol for the Chicago Board Options Exchange Volatility Index. Its nickname—"the fear gauge"—clearly tells us that it is a measure of risk. Through some complicated math, the VIX measures the level of volatility investors currently expect for stock prices over the following month and expresses it in the form of a single number. For example, at the start of 2007, before investors recognized the existence of the housing bubble, the VIX was about ten. By the start of the 2008, when the housing bubble concept was sinking in, the VIX had risen to about 30. In late October, 2008, after Fannie Mae and Freddie Mac were seized and the day after major brokerage firm Lehman Brothers declared bankruptcy, the VIX hit 80. It returned to ten, then recently exceeded 20 on concerns about rising interest rates and trade tensions.

The good news is that these three measures are highly correlated, so you can use any of them as a fair representation of current market risk. Two pictures will show the correlations among these measurement tools. First, the relationship between the investment-grade and high-yield bond spreads (Figure 5.1).

Using regression analysis (the statistical tool I described in chapter two), the two yield spreads were 66% correlated during the period shown. For economic data, that's quite a high correlation.

Figure 5.1. Close relationships exist between investment-grade and high-yield corporate bond risk spreads . . . (Sources: Investment-grade bond rate—Moody's. High-yield bond rate—Merrill Lynch. 10-year Treasury bond rate—Fed.)

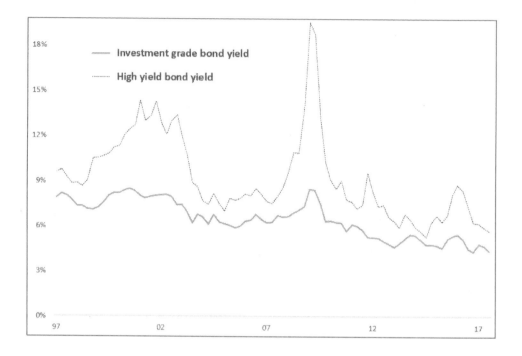

Second, are bond investors from Venus and stock investors from Mars, or do they view business risk similarly? Let's compare the investment grade yield spread with the VIX, shall we? On to Figure 5.2.

Figure 5.2. . . . And between perceived bond and stock risks. (Sources: Investment grade bond yield—Moody's. 10-year Treasury bond yield—Fed. VIX index—Chicago Board of Trade.)

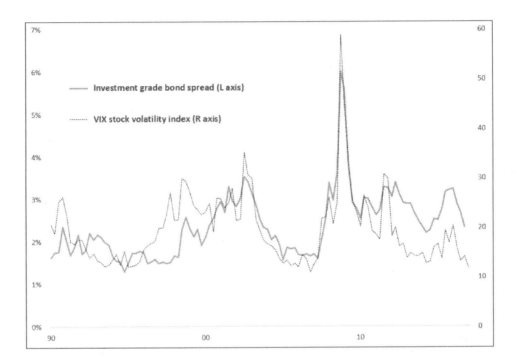

Once again, a close relationship—a 50% R^2.

We can safely conclude that, at any given time, investors have one general view of market risk, which they express similarly in the investment-grade bond, high-yield bond, and stock markets. We can now move on to analyzing why investors' views on market risk change over time.

Measuring Market Risks: Default Rates

FIGURE 5.3 MAKES IT PRETTY CLEAR that defaults, or bankruptcies, are the market risk that investors fear the most. A default means that bond investors stop getting interest payments and don't get all of their principal back. Investors also fear that a default increase will cause lenders to pull back on credit extension, with dire implications for the economy as a whole.

Figure 5.3. Investor risk is largely driven by loan default rate expectations, shown here for bond investors . . . (Sources: Investment grade bond yield—Moody's. 10-year Treasury bond yield—Fed. Loan charge-off rate—Fed.)

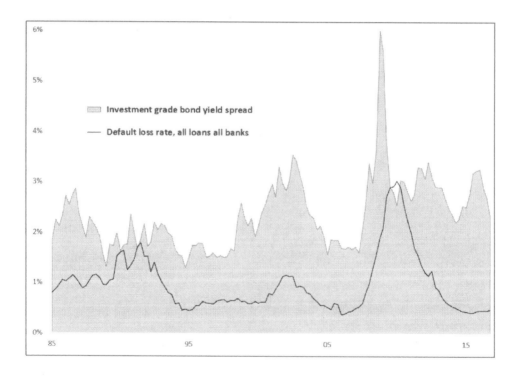

When loan defaults rise, stock investors suffer losses, and rising defaults in one sector generally mean lower earnings in other sectors as well.

So stock market performance is linked to changing default rates too, as Figure 5.4 shows.

Figure 5.4. . . . And here for stock investors. (Sources: S&P stock index—Yahoo Finance. Loan charge-off rate—Fed.)

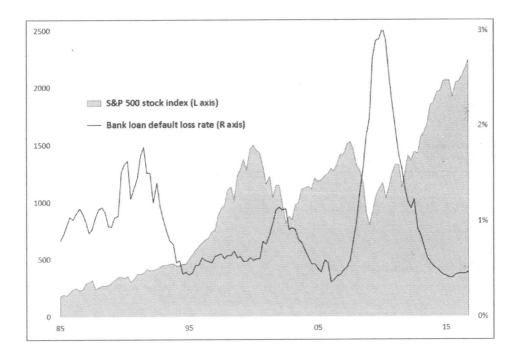

The major exception to the link between stock market changes and defaults was during the 1980s. The reason was that lenders kept actively lending very late into the default rate rise. As late as 1989, private debt growth still exceeded 4%.

Loan defaults don't just magically show up; something causes them. That something is an excessive increase in the amount of debt outstanding. Figures 5.5 and 5.6 show the relationship between excessive debt growth and defaults for the two main buckets of private sector debt—business loans and home mortgages.

Figure 5.5. Debt growth cycles in turn drive loan loss cycles, though with a long time lag. Here is the evidence for business loans . . . (Sources: Business debt—Fed. GDP—BEA. Loan charge-off rate—Fed.)

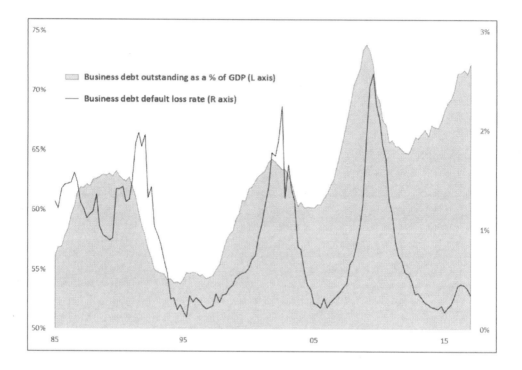

Figure 5.6. . . . And here is the evidence for home mortgage loans. (Sources: Home mortgage debt—Fed. GDP—BEA. Loan charge-off rate—Fed.)

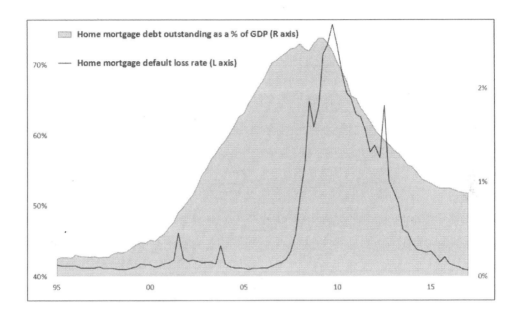

So to forecast the direction of perceived market risk, we need to keep a careful eye on the growth of private sector debt, measured as a percentage of GDP.

One final twist. Take a look at Figure 5.7, which compares the VIX index to the ratio between private sector debt outstanding and GDP.

Figure 5.7. Private sector debt growth is a key driver of the VIX stock risk measure. But clearly not the only one. (Sources: Debt data—Fed. Inflation—BLS. VIX index—Chicago Board of Exchange.)

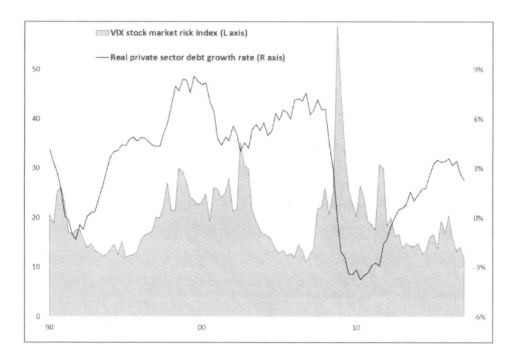

You can see that, from 1990 to about 2003, as the private sector debt ratio changed, so did the VIX—as my debt growth cycle theory would predict. But then the two delinked. While debt soared in the mid-2000s, the VIX actually declined. The VIX did catch up again in the 2008 financial crisis, only to delink again in recent years with debt rising and the VIX declining. Clearly, another major driver is at work.

Lucky for you, I am here to explain. The missing link is our old pal the Federal Reserve. By 2003, it became clear to investors that the Federal Reserve had committed to supporting debt growth. It did so at first by lowering interest rates; then, beginning in 2009, by buying bonds for its own account. So in estimating perceived market risk, we have to pay attention to *two* factors—the debt cycle and Federal Reserve policy.

On to the final variable in the earnings yield formula: the opportunity for earnings growth.

Understanding Earnings Growth

COMPANY EARNINGS GROWTH HAS A POWERFUL IMPACT on stock values, and therefore on the relative valuation of stocks versus bonds and cash. But before I talk about earnings growth, let's get clear *what* is growing.

Whole books have been written about the subject of business earnings, but you and I are busy people with a lot of Netflix to watch before the sun sets. So here are the highlights.

The term *business earnings* refers to the profit generated by a company—basically, company revenues minus expenses. Pretty obvious. But three business earnings facts are important for investors to understand.

First, the key metric for business earnings is earnings per share (EPS). American Airlines reported $1.9 billion in earnings in 2017. Cool! But what matters is not the whole $1.9 billion, but my *share* of that hoard. In 2017, American Airlines averaged 492 million shares of stock outstanding. So the company's EPS was $1.9 billion divided by 492 million, or $3.90 per share. If I own one share, the number of importance to me is not $1.9 billion, but $3.90.

Note that EPS can grow in one of two ways—increased earnings or fewer outstanding shares. The higher earnings thing is obvious. The fewer shares, the fewer business partners you have to share profits with. An extreme example of the latter variable is a small lending company named World Acceptance that I used to follow when I was a stock analyst. Its 2015 earnings of $111 million were 21% better than four years earlier—pretty good. But its 2015 EPS of $11.90 was *111%* greater than four years earlier—

pretty awesome! Why the difference? Because World repurchased a huge 43% of its shares over those four years. Fewer shares outstanding drove the EPS figure much higher than the earnings growth alone would explain. American Airlines is also pursuing this strategy; it has reduced its share count by one-third since 2014.

By contrast, many other companies continually issue more shares, either to the public to raise capital for growth, or to employees as compensation. For example, Salesforce.com added 24% more shares of stock from 2013 to 2017 through employee stock grants. Of course, increasing the share count depresses EPS growth.

Second, stocks are generally valued on current operating earnings, not reported earnings. Operating earnings are calculated without including revenues or expenses that are unlikely to recur in the future. For that reason, operating earnings is regarded as a better indicator of the company's likely future earnings. Since the value of a stock is very largely based on its expected future earnings stream, investors focus on current operating earnings rather than reported earnings.

For example, going back to American Airlines, its 2017 earnings included $712 million of one-time expenses due to completing its 2013 merger with US Air, restructuring its fleet and unusual labor costs. After deducting the $712 million, American's 2017 operating EPS was $4.81, not the $3.90 reported number.

Third, a company can use its earnings in a variety of ways. It can:

- Invest in new equipment, new products and new business lines
- Pay back debt
- Buy another company in an attempt to grow earnings faster or to diversify in order to increase stability
- Buy back stock, as I discussed above.
- Pay a dividend. This is the cash-in-the-investor's-pocket use of earnings. Dividends are usually higher at more mature and stable companies. For example, McDonald's paid $3.83 per share in

dividends out of its $5.71 in EPS during 2017, while Google paid no dividend while earning $32.25 per share.

- Retain earnings for use another day. For example, that's largely what Facebook has done with its earnings to date. At the end of 2017, it sat on $42 billion of cash, up from $11 billion four years earlier. Facebook will eventually use those retained earnings in one of the other ways I've listed.

Each of these uses of earnings generally benefits shareholders in one way or another, so just relying on operating earnings and ignoring the use of those earnings is usually fine. Note that I said "generally" benefits in the prior sentence because the ways some companies use their earnings have proven to be seriously misguided. Some companies keep buying back their stock even when it is clearly overvalued. Others invest in ill-conceived new business ideas. But the most common mistake is stupid acquisitions. For example, Microsoft bought the phone business of Nokia in 2014 for $7 billion. One year later—I repeat, *one year later!*—it wrote off the *entire* purchase price, plus another $2 billion in restructuring costs. A series of similarly foolish acquisitions contributed to the fact that for the 15 years from 1998 to 2013, Microsoft's stock price was flat.

Needless to say, the efficient use of capital is a critical way of judging the competence of corporate management. But that's a topic worthy of another book.

Expected Earnings Growth and Investment Values

EXPECTED GROWTH IN OPERATING EPS is a powerful creator of value for stocks. One easy way to see this is by comparing the ratio of price to earnings (or the P/E ratio) for stocks with different expected EPS growth rates. The faster the expected future EPS growth, the higher the P/E ratio. This explains why, in mid-2018, Target Stores' stock price sold at 13 times its expected 2018 EPS (a 13 P/E), while Amazon's sold at a 128 P/E! The difference in P/E ratios reflects the fact that investor expectations of future growth for Amazon are much higher than for Target. But I bet you knew that.

Companies' changing growth prospects over time are similarly reflected in changing P/E ratios. Look at how Wal-Mart's P/E ratio has declined over time as it has matured and its EPS growth rate has slowed (Figure 5.8).

Figure 5.8. Investors pay for earnings growth. Look at how Wal-Mart's P/E ratio declined as it matured and its EPS growth rate slowed. (Sources: Wal-Mart earnings—company reports. S&P 500 stock index—Yahoo Finance. S&P 500 EPS—Standard & Poor's.)

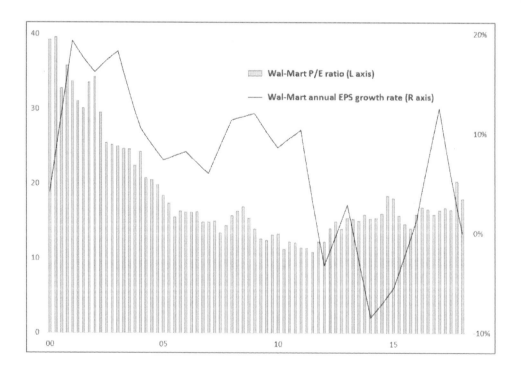

As you can imagine, identifying the economic variables that drive EPS growth is a pretty useful exercise for anyone hoping to forecast the future direction of the stock market. Let's tackle that assignment next.

What Drives EPS Growth?

GROWTH IN US BUSINESS EARNINGS LOGICALLY should be correlated to US GDP growth. Sure enough, the data shows that's the case (Figure 5.9).

Figure 5.9. Business earnings growth is highly correlated to GDP growth. (Sources: GDP—BEA. S&P 500 EPS—Standard & Poor's.)

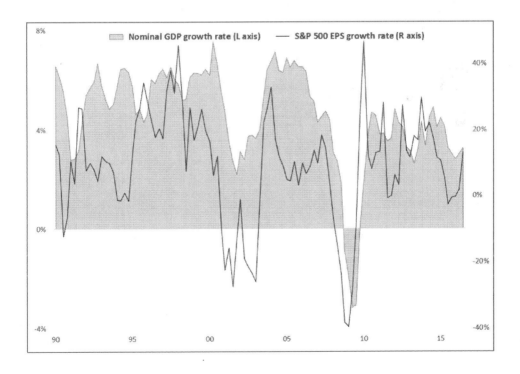

But notice in Figure 5.9 that while earnings growth and GDP growth are correlated, over the past three decades earnings growth was stronger by far. The GDP scale on the left goes up to only 8%, while the earnings growth scale goes up to 40%. Earnings growth has two other drivers that are independent of US GDP and that super-charged GDP growth. One is international sales. A greater share of US business sales and earnings comes from overseas than a decade or two ago. For example, in 2017, 63% of Apple's sales were overseas, compared to 50% two decades ago. The other is business profit margins. They have grown over time, as a calculation of the share of national income (a version of GDP; trust me on this one) going to business profits in Figure 5.10 shows.

Figure 5.10. Business profit margins improved over the past few decades, aiding profit and stock price growth. (Source—BEA).

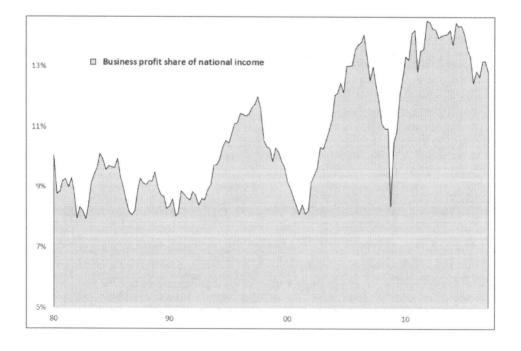

Why the increase in business profit margins over the past three decades? I believe there are three main reasons.

First, the balance of power between capital and labor has shifted toward capital. Growing imports and more widespread technology use favors employers over employees, as I noted in the my inflation discussion. The increase in profit margins is directly correlated to labor's decreased share of national income. Remember the "Greed is good" line made famous by Michael Douglas, playing Wall Street wheeler-dealer Gordon Gekko in the 1987 movie *Wall Street*? When he delivered that line, Gekko was at work on a scheme to gut the workforce of an airline. The Gekko character cartoonishly represents plenty of real-life business executives who direct company restructurings that include employee layoffs and shifts of jobs to overseas locales with far lower labor costs. The result is a greater share of corporate revenues going to profits. Thirty years after the movie's release, the trend continues.

Second, investors have gotten more aggressive in demanding higher profits from companies. That behavior began in earnest back in the 1980s, when the junk bond market developed, allowing "corporate raiders" to buy companies and restructure. Now the restructurings are largely driven by private equity and activist investment funds. Both types of funds focus on buying companies that they believe they can make more profitable, by reducing expenses, merging with competitors or selling parts of the business. Private equity funds are now investing north of $500 billion a year, and have well over $1 trillion of cash available to invest. Activist hedge funds are now demanding various management changes at more than 300 public companies at any given time.

Third, consolidation that has occurred in many industries. While free markets are all well and good in theory, they often stink for investors because a level playing field means lots of competition and therefore lower profit margins. Industry consolidation reduces the number of competitors, which often increases profit margins.

The airline industry is a good example of an industry that competed itself into several decades of serial bankruptcies beginning in the 1980s, but which has since consolidated into a much smaller number of rational players, each with a better shot at profitability. The railroad industry went through a similar transition. And check out the battery business. According to *The Wall Street Journal* (April 17, 2018), "Duracell and Energizer control close to 80% of the U.S. alkaline-battery market, according to Nielsen data provided by Jefferies, and that share is likely to grow. In January, Energizer announced plans to acquire No. 3 company, Rayovac..." What are they doing with this dominant position? *The Journal* notes that "Batteries on average cost 8.2% more than a year ago . . . " Lesson: Get yourself an oligopoly.

Conclusion: Speaking broadly, changes in the average growth rate of stock prices are largely driven by changes in loan default rates, GDP growth, and business profit margins.

6 How Debt Growth Drives Economic Cycles

TABLE 6.1 BRINGS TOGETHER THE EIGHT ECONOMIC DRIVERS of the variables in the earnings yield formulas we identified in the previous two chapters.

Table 6.1. The components of the earnings yield formula (column 1) and the corresponding economic drivers (columns 2 and 3).

Earnings yield formula components	Debt cycle drivers	Independent drivers
Time value of money:	Federal funds rate	
Inflation:	Lender willingness to lend	Wages Import volume Oil prices
Business risk:	Loan defaults	
Earnings growth:	GDP growth	Business profit margins

Is there a common theme for all eight of these economic drivers? Alas, no; life is too messy for that. But I'll show in this chapter that four of the economic drivers are linked by what I call the *debt cycle*. They appear in the column headed "Debt Cycle Drivers" in Table 6.1.

Let's start the debt cycle discussion with a look at actual US total debt facts. Table 6.2 is a snapshot of total debt outstanding as of the end of 2017.

Table 6.2. US debt outstanding (in trillions) at the end of 2017. (Source: Fed.)

U.S. total debt	**$49.1**
Household debt	**$15.3**
Home mortgages	10.1
Credit cards	1.0
Auto loans	1.1
Student loans	1.5
Other consumer credit	1.5
Business debt	**$14.3**
Commercial & industrial loans	10.2
Commercial mortgages	4.1
Government debt	**$19.5**
Federal	16.5
State and local	3.1

Nearly $50 trillion of debt. Our Founding Fathers must be so proud.

Debt Growth Is Cyclical

FIGURE 6.1 PRESENTS A HISTORY of the real (adjusted for inflation) growth rate of total debt going back to 1960.

Figure 6.1. Real debt growth cycles since 1960. (Sources: Debt data—Fed. Inflation—BLS.)

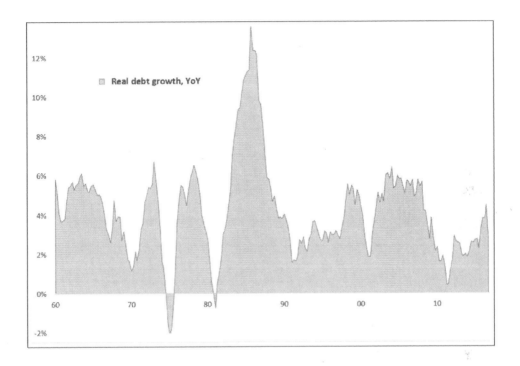

Debt cycles are a critical factor to consider when you're deciding whether to underweight or overweight stocks in your portfolio. Figures 6.2 and 6.3 should help you see why. They compare the growth rates of private sector (household and business) debt to the S&P 500 stock index, adjusted for inflation to make it easier to compare over time. For readability, I break the history of this relationship into two graphs, one covering the period from 1980 to 1990 and one covering the period from 1990 forward. Note that I use private sector debt, as opposed to total debt, which includes the government. I have my reasons, which I present later. Promise. Or threat.

Figure 6.2. Private sector debt growth is a critical indicator of where the stock market is going. The 1980s relationship . . . (Sources: Debt data—Fed. Inflation— BLS. S&P 500 stock index—Yahoo Finance. 10-year Treasury bond rate—Fed.)

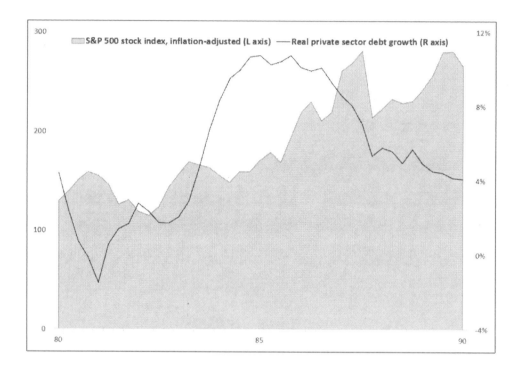

Figure 6.3. . . . And the relationship since 1990. (Sources: Debt data—Fed. Inflation—BLS. S&P 500 stock index—Yahoo Finance. 10-year Treasury bond rate—Fed.)

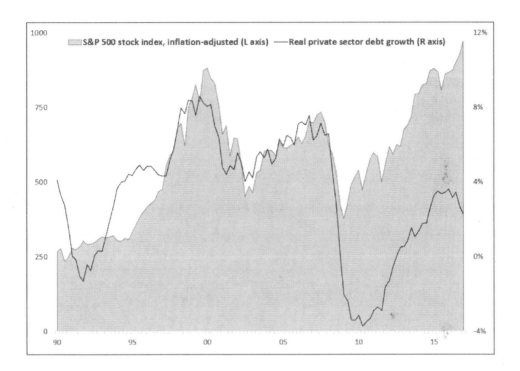

The close connection between debt growth and stock performance leads to my most important asset allocation rule: *If signs point to accelerating debt growth, overweight stocks. If signs instead suggest slowing debt growth ahead, underweight stocks by shifting towards bonds and/or cash.*

So a key challenge for us investors is to forecast changes in the rate of debt growth. Is it really possible to do that? Yes, it is. Read on, my skeptical friend.

How the Debt Cycle Works

THE STEPS IN THE DEBT CYCLE are shown in Figure 6.4 as a schematic.

Figure 6.4. The Debt Cycle.

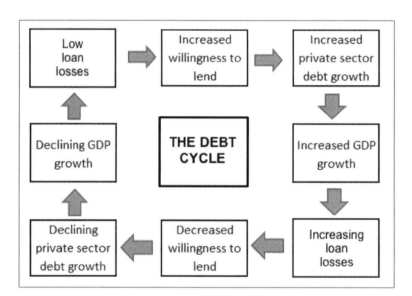

Because this is a cycle, I can start my analysis at any stage in the process and tell the story from there. I'll start at the stage in the cycle when bank loan losses are low, which is the upper left-hand box in the diagram. At this stage, low loan losses encourage banks to lend. The Federal Reserve measures banks' changing willingness to lend, as well as business and consumer willingness to borrow, in its periodic Senior Loan Officer's Opinion Survey. Figure 6.5 shows that banks' willingness to lend is a response to the level of default losses, our old friend from the business risk discussion.

Figure 6.5. Banks' willingness to lend logically changes in response to changes in loan default rates. (Source: Fed.)

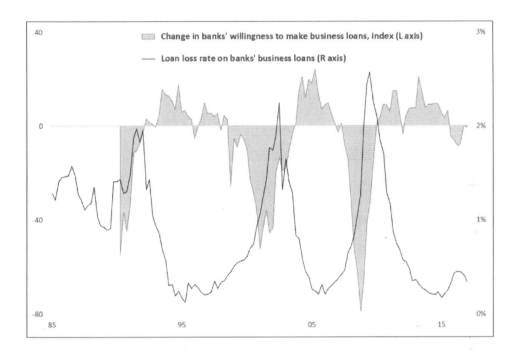

You can see that the willingness of banks to lend moves in the opposite direction to the bank charge-off rate, which measures the volume of default losses banks experience as a percent of the total loans they have invested in. For example, if a bank has $100 of loans outstanding, and a $5 loan defaults with the bank recovering only $3, the net $2 loss causes a 2% charge-off rate.

But wait—we're considering only lenders' willingness to lend. Debt creation requires two parties—a borrower and a lender. Why couldn't *borrowers'* willingness to take the lenders' proffered funds really drive the debt cycle?

To answer this question, let's start by recognizing that there are tens of millions of borrowers and tens of thousands of lenders in the US, and their individual motivations and decision strategies vary greatly. To understand how the overall debt cycle works, we have to generalize about the behaviors of this vast mass of decision-makers. With that caveat, the weight of proof clearly supports the generalization that lender behavior, not borrower behavior, drives debt cycles. Three arguments are particularly compelling: borrower logic, lender logic, and the willingness survey lead/lag. Let's consider them in turn.

Borrower Logic

HOW COULD THOSE TENS OF MILLIONS OF BORROWERS (homeowners, small business managers, credit card users, and others) act in concert? What would make them collectively say "Now it's time to borrow" at one stage in the cycle and "Enough borrowing already" at a different stage?

You might argue that people start borrowing after their financial circumstances improve, which would suggest that changes in borrowing activity should follow changes in jobs and personal income. This sounds logical—but the data actually shows that changes in borrowing tend to *precede* changes in jobs and personal income. I present the evidence later in this chapter. In reality, lots of people *always* want to borrow in order to buy more stuff.

Lender Logic

LENDERS, ON THE OTHER HAND, have a logical shared reason for collectively increasing or decreasing their lending activities—namely, the falling or rising levels of loan losses. Low loss levels make lending more profitable, while high loss levels make it more costly. The swings in earnings due to loan charge-off rate changes can be huge. For example, credit card company Discover earned $1.0 billion in operating income in 2006, but its earnings fell to $0.6 billion in 2007 and then to just $0.1 billion in 2008 as the Great Recession's toll of loan losses mounted. When the economy recovered fully in 2011, loan losses dropped, and Discover's operating earnings zoomed to $2.2 billion.

It's natural that lenders are more eager to lend money when that activity is highly profitable, which helps to explain why the two lines in Figure 6.6 above move in tandem.

Lender Behavior Changes Precede Borrower Changes

THE FEDERAL RESERVE'S SENIOR LOAN OFFICER'S OPINION SURVEY handily measures both lenders' changing willingness to lend and business and consumer willingness to borrow. Figure 6.6 compares the history of both trends.

Figure 6.6. An increase in banks' willingness to supply small businesses with credit generally precedes small businesses' demand for credit. (Source: Fed.)

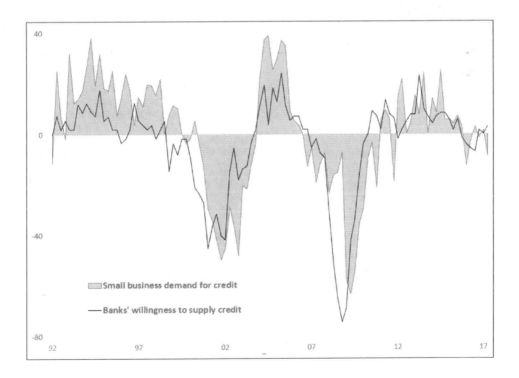

Figure 6.6 shows that lender attitudes usually change a little before borrower attitudes. This means that, as investors seeking to forecast future changes in the debt cycle, it is best to track lender behavior, not borrower behavior.

We're now ready for the next box in the debt cycle schematic. What happens when banks are more willing to make loans (as in the top center box in the diagram)? Not surprisingly, they actually lend more, as Figure 6.7 shows.

Figure 6.7. Oddly enough, when banks want to lend, they typically do. (Sources: Debt data—Fed. Inflation—BLS. Bank willingness to lend—Fed.)

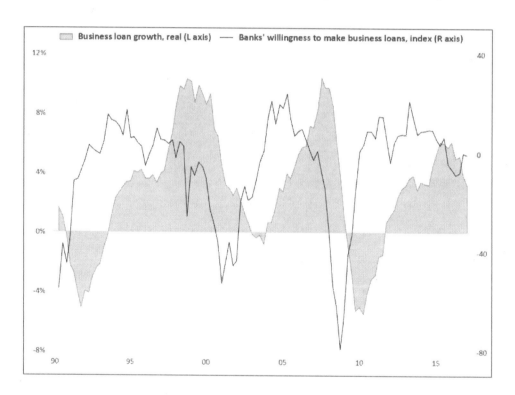

Now for the most important part of the cycle: the stage in which debt growth drives cyclical GDP growth (the top right and center right boxes in Figure 6.4). Figure 6.8 makes the correlation quite clear.

Figure 6.8. Debt growth drives GDP growth. This fact is the single most important key to debt cycle investing. (Sources: GDP—BEA. Debt data—Fed. Inflation—BLS.)

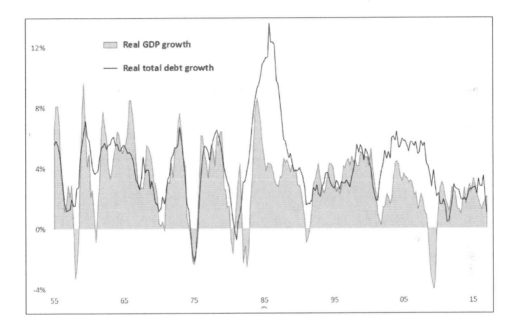

Note that debt growth doesn't *precede* GDP growth; instead, changes in the two growth patterns are simultaneous. That is because borrowers typically spend their borrowed cash almost immediately. I take out an auto loan to buy a car *now*; the government borrows money by selling bonds to meet *current* spending obligations; a business owner uses funds from her revolving credit account to make an *immediate* purchase of equipment she needs, and so on. To borrow is to spend.

And who doesn't like to spend more? Pretty much nobody. Therefore, few people try to restrain debt growth once it has started. In fact, providing plausible public excuses for more debt growth is a highly-paid profession. Consider the outpouring of "expert" opinion that the $1.5 trillion of borrowing required to fund the 2017 tax cut will spur so much growth that the borrowing won't be needed. (Fat chance, but that's another story.)

The lack of restraint by responsible parties who should (or do) know better encourages easier and easier lending terms, which in turn cause loan losses to rise. For example, for several decades, a number of local banks made home mortgage loans to people with subprime credit scores, but only if that borrower could make a 30% or 40% down payment. By the peak of the housing bubble in 2006, the down payment requirement for subprime home mortgage borrowers fell to as low as 10%. And barely a peep from government regulators and well-known economists.

Figure 6.9 shows that sharp increases in the loan growth rate are eventually followed by an increase in loan charge-offs.

Figure 6.9. Too-fast loan growth inevitably leads to rising loan losses, as this history of business lending shows. (Sources: Debt data—Fed. Inflation—BLS. Bank charge-off rate—Fed.

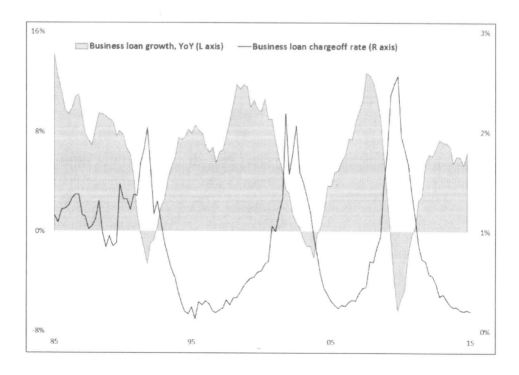

I bet you can figure out how the rest of the debt cycle works. A rise in loan losses reduces banks' willingness to lend, which reduces debt growth, which reduces GDP growth. Loan losses then eventually decline, and we have made it all the way back to the starting point in the cycle.

The broad outline of the private sector debt cycle shown in Figure 6.4 has proven to be a powerful tool to guide investment decisions. Take a look at Figure 6.10, which compares the business loan loss rate cycle to the S&P 500 since 1990. Note that I inverted the loss rate because low loss rates are good and higher rates are bad. A terrific correlation—stocks move with the debt cycle.

Figure 6.10. The stock market moves in sync with the debt cycle. Memorize that fact. (Sources: Bank business loan loss rate—Fed. S&P 500—Yahoo Finance.)

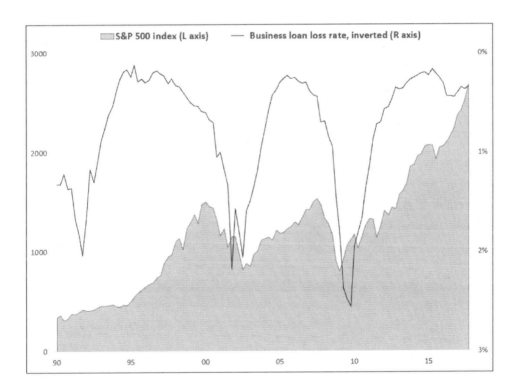

The Role of Government in Debt Growth

I HAVE A CONFESSION TO MAKE. I haven't yet told you the whole story of the debt cycle. So far, I've tracked only private sector debt activity, leaving out the government. How can one miss a whole government, especially one as cute as ours? How could I have abused your child-like trust in me? But let's somehow learn from this and move on.

In fact, the government has an important role to play in the debt cycle—to minimize the impact of private sector lending mistakes. That can be seen in Figure 6.11. It shows two debt cycles—one for the private sector only, and one for total debt, including government debt.

Figure 6.11. Government debt growth has served to moderate the wide swings in private-sector debt growth.

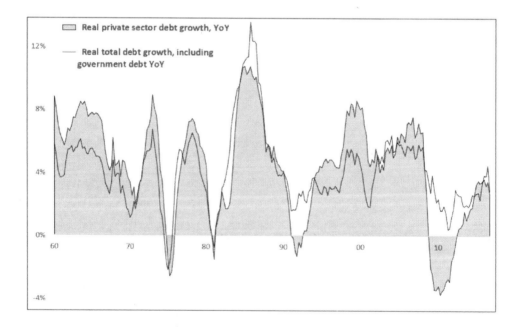

You can see from Figure 6.11 that the government has acted as a moderator, lowering the highs of private-sector debt growth and, most important, raising the lows. For example, the collapse of private-sector lending during 2008-2009 would have caused a depression, not simply a serious recession, without the surge in government borrowing.

So if I were to be entirely accurate (it can't hurt every once in a while), the debt cycle graphic should include government borrowing, as shown in Figure 6.12.

Figure 6.12. The debt cycle schematic, including government debt.

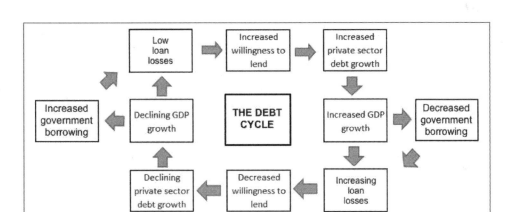

Notice the two new boxes that appear in Figure 6.12 that did *not* appear in Figure 6.4. Increased GDP growth generally leads to decreased government borrowing. Similarly, declining GDP growth generally leads to increased government borrowing.

Why Do Debt Cycles Occur?

YOU'VE NOW SEEN WHAT THE WHOLE DEBT CYCLE LOOKS LIKE, and the impact this cycle has on the overall economy. But why does it work that way? Why the repeated pattern of booms and busts in debt growth and loan losses? After all, lenders are business people, and business people are rational creatures, right? That means they must follow rational rules when they underwrite loans, right? And if that's the case, why should loan losses ever become unacceptably high, forcing lenders to reverse their lending practices?

Quite logical, but quite wrong. Assuming rational economic behavior is one of those common errors I discussed in chapter one. Experience shows that business people are not highly rational creatures. In fact, "kinder-gartners with attention deficit disorder" is often a more accurate description.

A rational person looking at the potential growth rate of any business first sizes up the purchasing power of the customer base for their product. In business school, it's called market research. Let's apply some market research to the business of lending.

For consumer lending, a logical purchasing power constraint on borrowing capacity is household income. The more money I make, the greater my capacity to service debt. US households' capacity to repay debt grows in step with the growth rate of their *disposable personal income* (DPI). As measured by the Bureau of Economic Analysis, DPI includes wages, investment income, small business income, and benefits payments from the government (Social Security, Medicare, and so on). For business lending, a reasonable capacity constraint is the earnings growth of the business customers, and a rough estimate for tracking earnings growth is GDP growth.

Think of these two growth constraints as the rational *speed limits* on lending. Lenders can safely grow their loan books roughly in line with the speed limit growth rates for household income and corporate earnings.

How well have lenders adhered to those speed limits over time? I'll bet you can guess. A lot of reckless driving. A lot of accidents in the left lane. Let's slow down and rubberneck a little.

Housing Bubbles: Reckless Home Mortgage Lending

FIGURE 6.13 COMPARES HOME MORTGAGE DEBT GROWTH to household income (DPI) growth.

Figure 6.13. Home mortgage debt growth has frequently exceeded its speed limit, household income growth—often by significant amounts. (Sources: Household income—BEA. Debt data—Fed.)

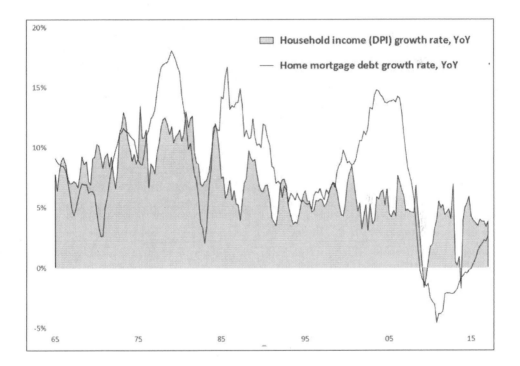

Figure 6.13 shows three eras when home mortgage lenders *grossly* exceeded their speed limit:

- The late 1970s. Back then, the excess lending was centered in the housing markets of the oil states following the 1970s surge in oil prices. It ended with particularly nasty housing corrections in Texas, Oklahoma, and Alaska.

- The mid-1980s. This time, the bubble occurred in the coastal states, particularly in California and New England. Both of those regions suffered subsequent housing busts.

- The mid-2000s. This Big Mama of home mortgage lending bubbles was national. Big Mama spawned two bubble babies. One bubble was substantial speculative home construction; when the Great Recession began in 2007, a record 1.5 million more homes than normal were sitting empty. The other bubble was a massive refinancing wave that allowed homeowners to turn $2 trillion of their housing equity savings into cash for spending from 2002 through 2007.

Housing bubbles are particularly hard to stop because so many people enjoy them: home builders, realtors, mortgage lenders, speculators who buy homes for short-term resale, bankers, Wall Street financiers, and, most important of all, the more than 60% of households that own their homes and benefit from home price appreciation.

In fact, it's hard to think of anyone unhappy with a housing bubble *while it's in process*. Worriers are not deemed prophets, but rather "deficit scolds," a term coined by the economist and *New York Times* columnist Paul Krugman. After the bubble bursts, of course, it's a different story. Then it's about assigning blame to someone other than yourself.

Credit Card Bubbles: Reckless Consumer Lending

CREDIT CARD LENDING WENT ON A TEAR from the mid-1980s to about 2000, as Figure 6.14 shows.

Figure 6.14. Credit card debt growth versus its personal income speed limit. (Sources: Household income—BEA. Debt data—Fed.

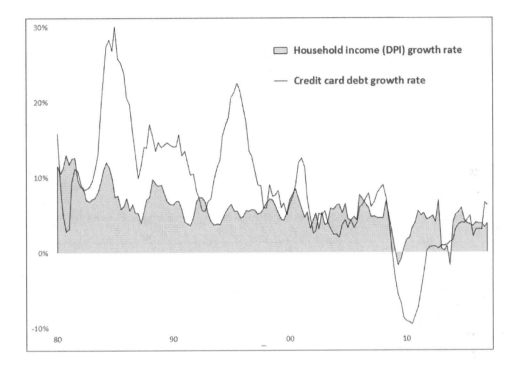

In the 1970s and 1980s, credit cards were still an immature product; only $132 billion of credit card debt was outstanding at the end of 1985. But in the late 1980s, a number of credit card issuers, including new entrants like Capital One, Providian, and Advanta, created new credit card underwriting tools using what we call today "big data." Of course the new tools were used to excess. From 1985-2000, credit card debt growth above the rate of household income growth added $270 billion to households' spending. The lending surge lead to soaring credit card defaults by the mid-1990s even without a recession. A major industry shakeout followed.

Business Lending Bubbles: Reckless Lending to Companies

FIGURE 6.15 COMPARES BUSINESS (NON-MORTGAGE) DEBT GROWTH to nominal GDP growth, which I'll use as a rough proxy for business revenues.

Figure 6.15. Business lending growth and its GDP growth speed limit. (Sources: GDP—BEA. Debt data—Fed.)

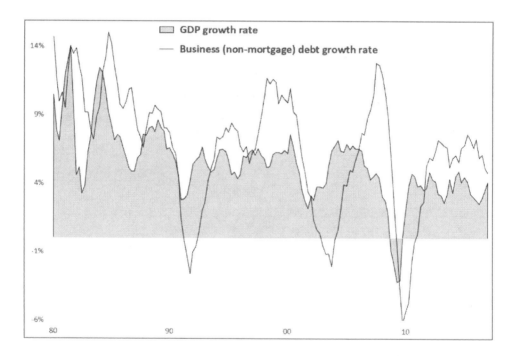

Each of the four business lending bubbles during the past four decades had its own charms:

- The bubble of the mid-1980s was centered on the emergence of junk bonds (described in chapter two). What started out as an innovative and productive lending niche inevitably turned into too much of a good thing, as speculators used junk debt to make high-risk company acquisitions and to fund companies with shaky business models.

- The bubble of the late-1990s featured lending to finance the initial build-out of the Internet infrastructure—a good idea, but one that inevitably became overheated as billions were poured into huge excess capacity.

- The bubble of the mid-2000s saw a boom in *leveraged buyouts* (LBOs)—company acquisitions by private equity firms using as much debt as possible to make the purchases. Many of these debt-laden LBOs went bust. The 2017 bankruptcy of Toys "R" Us is an example.

- The bubble of the 2010s has seen investment-grade companies take advantage of record low interest rates to borrow money to buy back their own stock, which increases earnings per share and in turn usually increases stock prices. This lending has actually been more benign than most other excessive lending because the borrowers have more financial resources, but there is always the risk of overconfidence leading to excesses.

Business lenders don't seem to be quick learners; they still seem ready to jump into a big new arena for reckless lending about once every decade.

An Industry Over-Lending Example: Energy Companies

OIL PRICES STARTED A MAJOR RISE IN 2006, in large part due to rapidly growing demand from China. Strong demand made energy companies creative; they developed the technology behind fracking as a way of extracting oil and gas from previously unpromising locations. Buying drilling sites and building out the fracking infrastructure required capital, and debt investors were happy to supply it, as Figure 6.16 shows.

Figure 6.16. A recent history of the issuance of high-yield energy industry debt illustrates the standard boom/bust lending cycle. (Source: S&P Global Market Intelligence.

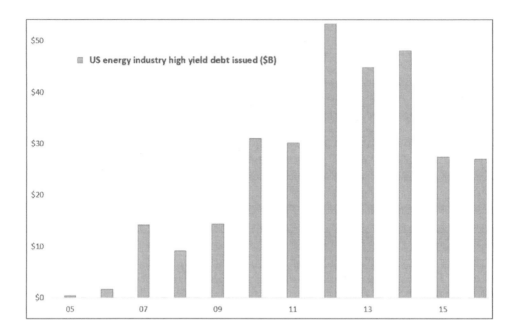

But guess what? Energy companies created too much of a good thing. US oil production nearly doubled from 2007 to 2015, creating an oil glut that drastically drove down prices. Many fracking projects became uneconomic, and lots of that high-yield debt went into arrears. And energy company high-yield debt issuance shrank. In other words, standard bubble protocol.

Asset-Backed Lenders: The Most Reckless Drivers of All

WHILE THE BANKS HAVE HAD THEIR PERIODS OF IRRATIONALITY, in recent decades non-bank lenders proved to be far crazier. Non-bank lending is mostly in the form of asset-backed (mostly, mortgage-backed) securities, debt products that I described in chapter four.

Non-bank lenders have done a far worse job than banks in managing risks, as the next two pictures illustrate. Figure 6.17 shows that non-bank commercial real estate mortgage lending surged from 1998 to 2008, supporting well-above-speed-limit growth in commercial real estate debt.

Figure 6.17. The advent of financing commercial mortgages through mortgage-backed securities ultimately caused significant overlending. (Sources: GDP—BEA. Debt data—Fed.)

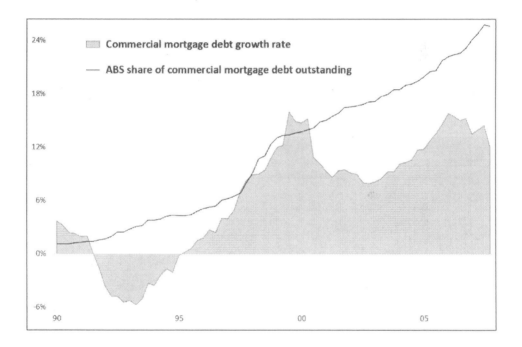

The excess lending was used partly for excess real estate construction, but most of it was used to help commercial real estate owners pay ever-higher prices for properties or to take out cash for themselves. The extra building and the increased financial leverage inevitably caused a spike in charge-off rates (Figure 6.18).

Figure 6.18. The commercial mortgage lending boom driven by asset-backed securities of course ended badly. (Source: Fed.)

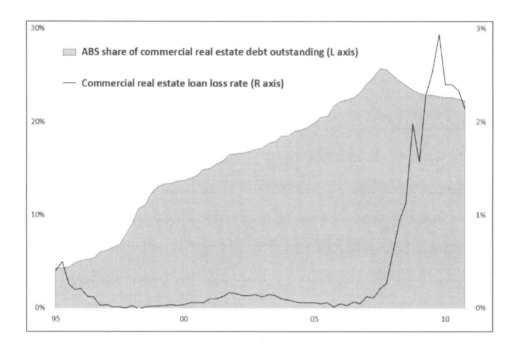

Where Does the Bubble Money Go?

THIS QUESTION COULD BE INTERPRETED—and answered—in several ways. Here are three of interest.

Where is the bubble debt spent? It is primarily spent on infrastructure, broadly defined. The World Bank tracks capital spending, which they say includes "land improvements; plant, machinery, and equipment purchases; and the construction of roads and railways, and [real estate] . . . " Look at how closely the World Bank's measure of infrastructure spending, as a percentage of GDP, correlated to debt growth in the US (Figure 6.19).

Figure 6.19. Debt bubbles generally fund capital spending booms in real estate, business equipment, and infrastructure. (Sources: Debt—Fed. Inflation—BLS. CPI—BLS. Capital spending ratio—World Bank.)

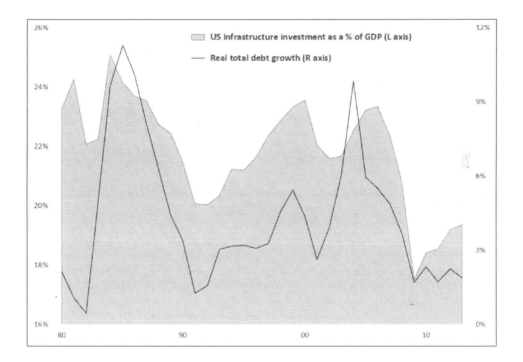

One clear sign of too much lending, then, is steep growth in residential and/or commercial real estate construction and/or spikes in spending on business equipment. And this relationship between debt and capital spending bubbles is quite evident in other countries, not only the US. I guess humans just like to build stuff.

How has the bubble debt been financed? How could debt growth have exceeded GDP growth for so much of the past 35 years? An important part of the answer: foreign investors. Figure 6.20 shows a history of the ownership of US debt, broken out between domestic and foreign investors.

Figure 6.20. Foreign investors have played a major role in financing America's debt bubbles. (Source—Fed.)

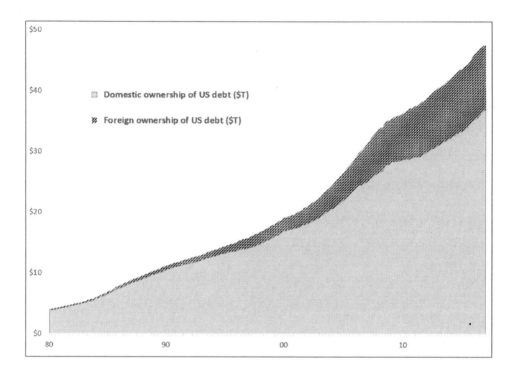

As you can see, foreigners now own about one quarter of US debt. Combine this fact with the surge in the trade deficit I noted, and the picture makes sense. Americans over the past 35 years purchased trillions of dollars' worth of foreign-made goods on a lay-away plan. I hope our kids enjoy paying for the junk we bought.

Who got rich from the debt bubbles? One group that certainly enjoyed the debt bubbles was Wall Street. I know, I was there. The more debt issued, the more Wall Street employees at brokerage firms, big banks, investment managers and the like got paid.

But it was even better than that. The issuance of plain vanilla debt—say, a new mortgage-backed security (MBS) issued through Fannie Mae—is not that profitable. But in the good old days of 2005, the issuance of a subprime MBS, with its higher yield to investors, was dramatically more profitable. In fact, the pace of issuance of asset-backed securities turns out to be a good indicator of Wall Street profits, as the example of Morgan Stanley illustrates (Figure 6.21).

Figure 6.21. Issuance of asset-backed securities (ABS) has been a key driver of Wall Street profits. (Sources: ABS issued—Fed. Morgan Stanley EPS—company reports.)

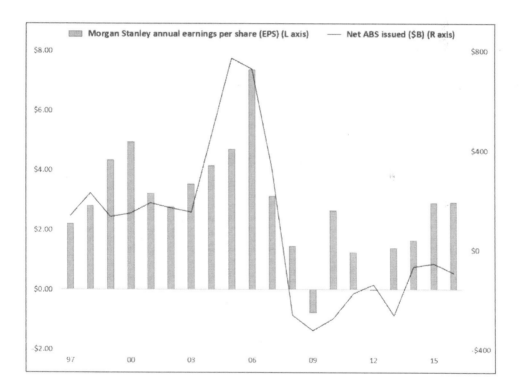

Investment tip: When your financial advisor pitches you on a clever new product, hang up the phone.

The Psychology of Bubbles and Busts

BUBBLE-AND-BUST CYCLES HAVE HAPPENED FOR CENTURIES, maybe millennia for all I know (note to self: write a book on debt financing in the Aztec Empire. Call Netflix about the movie rights.). Way back in the 1930s, economics legend John Maynard Keynes explained how human behavior creates bubbles. Keynes came up with the concept of "animal spirits," which he described this way:

> Most, probably, of our decisions to do something positive, the full consequences of which will be drawn out over many days to come, can only be taken as the result of animal spirits—a spontaneous urge to action rather than inaction, and not as the outcome of a weighted average of quantitative benefits multiplied by quantitative probabilities. (*The General Theory of Employment, Interest and Money*, Macmillan, 1936, pages 161-162.)

Sounds raw and primitive, and certainly not rational. But we see the same pattern in many areas of human behavior—surges of positive enthusiasm that end in excesses and pain. Think of that fourth bourbon shot. Or that double black diamond ski run. Maybe this is even how human progress works—not through reasonable, planned advances but in a fever of activity that produces an excess of new products and new ideas. The fever eventually breaks, leading to a shake-out and the restoration of a measure of rationality . . . until the next fever hits.

Lenders are humans just like you and me. (Okay, maybe they are more boring and more likely to wear chinos on weekends, but besides that . . .) And that means they are subject to the same attacks of animal spirits that Keynes identified, leading to results both positive and negative.

Why Don't You Hear More About the Debt Cycle?

THE HUMAN FOIBLES OF LENDERS, THEN, are the key reason for the recurrence of debt cycles. And while debt cycles vary in their details, with booms and busts of varying duration and intensity, the typical pattern is fundamentally consistent and therefore predictable.

If the debt cycle is as important as I say it is, both for tracking the economy and for making smart investment choices, why doesn't the media cover it continually? The answer hearkens back to four of the five weaknesses in our economic thinking I discussed in chapter one.

We fall for stories. Every debt bubble is sustained by one or more fables. Because spending more money by borrowing is fun, too many people are happy to believe any fable that justifies more spending. For example, the credit card bubble of the 1990s was based on the fable that lenders (the early adopters of big data) had turned credit analysis into a science. And the housing bubble of the 2000s was supported by the convenient, and errant, belief that home prices could never go down, and that increasing home ownership, as opposed to renting, could only be good for society.

We believe humans are largely rational economic beings. We can't imagine that bankers are as irrational as they often behave. We find it hard to accept that consumers and businesses can overborrow to the point of bankruptcy. Yet they do. All of the time. For example, in a good year, over 200,000 US companies and 800,000 US households declare bankruptcy.

We assume that today's trend is likely to continue indefinitely. This is particularly true when things are going well. In the midst of a debt bubble, it is the rare person that forecasts a downturn. As a former stock analyst, I can attest that only a handful of companies ever anticipate the unhappy ending that a debt bubble inevitably creates, and even fewer act on that realization.

Former CEO of Citigroup Chuck Prince displayed classic trend behavior during the early stages of the financial crisis. He told *The Financial Times* that the lending bubble would end at some point, but it would not be disrupted by the emerging turmoil in the US subprime mortgage market. He denied that Citigroup, one of the biggest providers of finance to private equity deals, was pulling back. "When the music stops, in terms of liquidity, things will be complicated. But as long as the music is playing, you've got to get up and dance. We're still dancing," he said (*Time*, July 10, 2007).

Yes indeed, things got "complicated." Citigroup's stock price when he spoke: $47. Citigroup stock price two years later: $5. That was one expensive dance.

We cling to our favorite theories. Economists have come up with many theories to explain economic cycles, most of which are more scientific-looking than my simple observation that they are driven largely by debt. Similarly, investors have come up with many asset allocation theories that seem a lot more exciting than tracking the growth rate of total debt. The next chapter debunks some of those theories. But as long as they continue to circulate, they attract followers who use them to justify ignoring debt cycles and their impact on the economy.

Debt Cycle Denial: The Reagan Economic "Miracle"

OUR HUMAN WILLINGNESS TO MISREAD REALITY for emotionally-driven reasons leads to what I call *debt cycle denial*—the willful act of averting one's eyes from the repeated tendency of the debt cycle to drive economic booms and busts.

An enduring economic myth that illustrates the power of debt cycle denial is the story of the Reagan economic "miracle." This fantasy was succinctly described by Wayne Allen Root of Breitbart News on July 16, 2016, in reacting to the economic promises of another Republican political leader: "Donald Trump just delivered the greatest Republican Presidential address since Reagan . . . The heart of Trump's speech was about using a combination of massive tax cuts and killing regulation to return America to prosperity—just like Reagan."

Millions of Americans share Root's belief that President Reagan ushered in a period of tremendous economic growth through the two simple acts Root mentioned—cutting taxes and reducing business regulation. This belief largely shapes conservative economic thinking to this day. For example, on July 14, 2017, *The Wall Street Journal* published an op-ed by Arthur Laffer and Stephen Moore, co-chairmen of the amusingly titled Committee to Unleash Prosperity, which lauded the economic growth of more than 4% enjoyed "during the go-go Reagan years," then drew the following policy conclusion:

> Governors and mayors should be lobbying nonstop for the tax cuts proposed by Mr. Trump, which would revitalize state finances. When the federal government cuts taxes, more money is left in the hands of businesses and workers. The Trump plan would free up an estimated $2 trillion to $4 trillion over 10 years—an enormous influx of cash for state and local economies.

I too once fervently believed the story of the Reagan economic miracle. Now the Reagan Administration did many admirable things: it raised national spirits, it killed off inflation, it helped bring down the USSR, and so on. But sadly, when I dug into the data, I found that the "Reagan economic miracle" turned out to be mostly a fable. To see why, look at Figure 6.22. It shows a history of total US debt outstanding as a percent of GDP. I then divided this history into presidential tenures.

Figure 6.22. The Reagan economic miracle, or the biggest debt bubble in US history? (Sources: GDP—BEA. Debt—Fed. Inflation—BLS.)

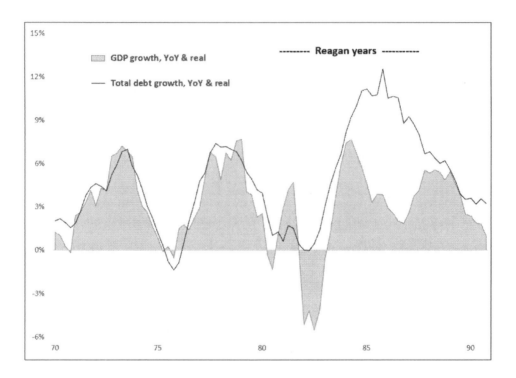

Yes, GDP growth was greater during Reagan's tenure than it had been during the previous decade. But this growth occured at the cost of a huge build-up in debt. A good deal of that debt blew up right after Reagan left office, when commercial real estate mortgages, junk bonds, and some home mortgage debt plummeted in value, creating hundreds of billions of dollars of loan losses. Widespread failures in the savings and loan industry as a result of that debt collapse ended up requiring a $200 billion federal government bailout in 1991, or over $350 billion in today's dollars

The Reagan myth boils down to this simple example: Let's say that last year you earned and spent $50,000. This year, you earned $50,000 again, but you spent $60,000 because you also borrowed $10,000. Your economic activity has increased significantly. You've piled up more stuff. But is that an economic miracle, or just a temporary boost based on borrowing that can't be sustained, and that you will have to pay for down the road?

ॐ

IN THIS CHAPTER, I'VE EXPLAINED THE IMPACT of the debt cycle on the overall economy, which explains why it is one of the key factors you need to consider when you're making asset allocation decisions. I've identified the crucial driver of the debt cycle—the changing attitudes of lenders. I've shown that lenders' willingness to lend is tied to the trend of loan losses incurred. And I've shown that this process quite often gets irrational.

I'm aware, however, that you may be wondering about a number of other well-known economic factors that could drive economic and investment cycles. Where are business decisions? Consumer confidence? Tax policy? The Federal Reserve? Turn the page and get your answers.

7 What *Doesn't* Drive Economic Cycles

IN A WORLD IN WHICH MOST OF US ARE DROWNING in far too much information to absorb, finding out what data we can safely ignore is almost as valuable as learning what we should know. This chapter is therefore devoted to telling you what economic data you *don't* have to pay much attention to when allocating your financial assets.

I said in the last chapter that lenders—bankers and related species—are the primary drivers of the debt cycle. In economic lingo, lender behavior is a *leading indicator*. Other factors in the economy get a lot more attention, but it turns out that most of them *follow* the lead of the lenders and the debt cycle—they are *lagging indicators*. These other, secondary factors include:

- Businesses—non-lender businesses, to be exact
- The Federal Reserve through its monetary policies
- Consumers
- Governmental policy, particularly tax policy

To oversimplify just a bit: The debt cycle drives the economy, and bankers are the stars of the story. The other players listed above have cameo roles.

I can hear you objecting already: "So you are seriously claiming that Mrs. Hernandez, my favorite loan officer at my neighborhood Pismo Beach National Bank branch, is more important to my investment returns than the CEO of Boeing? Or the chairman of the Federal Reserve? Or three hundred million consumers with trillions of dollars of spending power? Or even the evil empire IRS?"

Well, yes, it's true—not about Mrs. Hernandez per se, but about the lending industry as a whole. Let me show you why. I start with business activity.

Businesses Don't Drive Economic Cycles

IT CERTAINLY MAKES INTUITIVE SENSE that businesses drive economic cycles. After all, consider the crucial activities businesses perform. They hire and fire people. They invest—or don't invest—in new factories, new equipment, and new ideas. They build and shrink their inventories of raw materials and finished goods. They earn money and pay dividends to investors.

Those significant activities impact all of us every day. As President Calvin Coolidge famously said, "The business of America is business." But the data pretty clearly shows that *all of these activities actually lag GDP*. Which means that businesses don't *drive* economic cycles, they *respond* to them.

So sorry, guys and gals in suits. You aren't economic leaders, you're economic followers. But you do look sharp.

For proof, let's look first at job growth (Figure 7.1, on the next page).

Job growth and GDP growth are very well correlated, which makes common sense. But the chart shows that changes in hiring generally lag changes in GDP by a few quarters. Businesses evidently don't hire and fire *in anticipation* of a cyclical economic change; they adjust their workforces *in response* to changes in sales.

Figure 7.1. Business hiring lags GDP . . . (Sources: GDP—BEA. Inflation and jobs—BLS.)

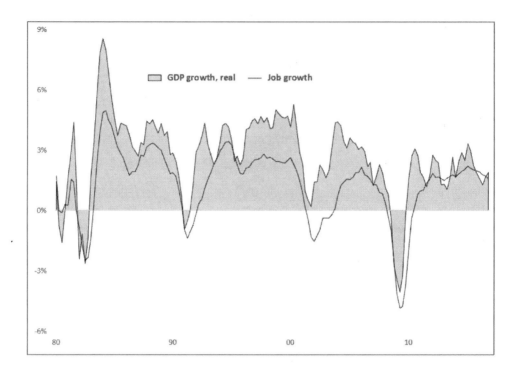

How about business investment, then? Take a look at Figure 7.2.

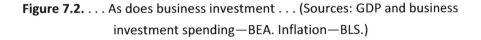

Figure 7.2. . . . As does business investment . . . (Sources: GDP and business investment spending—BEA. Inflation—BLS.)

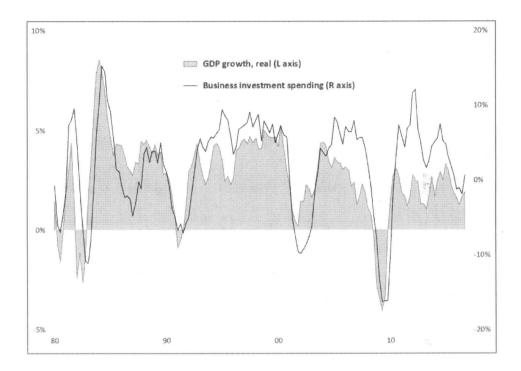

We see the same story here as with job growth: A good correlation, but business investment spending lags GDP changes by even a longer period of time than job growth does. This makes sense. A manufacturer receiving more orders adds a shift and new employees. Only when the factory is at full capacity does the manufacturer build a new facility.

Finally, let's look at changes in business inventories. At one time, business inventory cycles were seen by economists as one of the primary drivers of economic cycles. For example, economist Yi Wen wrote in a 2002 Cornell University working paper called "Understanding the Inventory Cycle" that "for many years economists have speculated that understanding inventory fluctuations may provide the key to understanding the business cycle."

But Figure 7.3 shows that, while the relationship between inventory changes and economic cycles indeed is quite close, this business activity is driven by the broader economic cycle rather than vice versa.

Figure 7.3. . . . As do changes in business inventory. (Sources: GDP and business inventory growth—BEA. Inflation—BLS.)

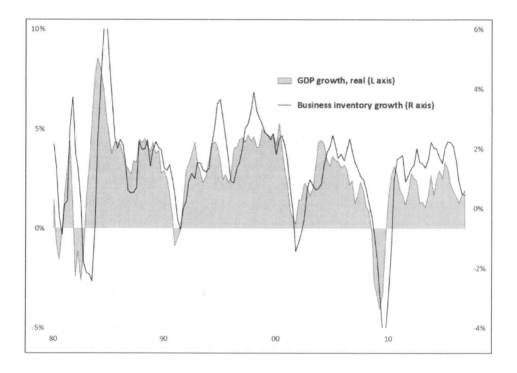

Yi Wen ends up agreeing with me: "I also show that the inventory cycle and the business cycle are intimately related by sharing a common source of uncertainty—consumption demand . . . " We agree because I've shown that demand for goods and services at the margin is driven by debt growth—

which in turn drives more consumer spending and inventory stocking (business spending).

Here's an anecdote that helped me understand business behavior and its relationship to economic cycles. In 2006, I attended an investor meeting with the CEO of Liz Claiborne, the women's fashion company. Someone asked the executive why his company's sales had been so strong the year before. The CEO thought for a minute and finally replied, "I don't know."

This honest answer speaks volumes about business behavior. Business managers are not seers who can infallibly predict the future. Rather, the customer either buys or doesn't buy. Then management responds.

Federal Reserve Interest Rate Policies Don't Drive Economic Cycles

THE MEMBERS OF THE FEDERAL RESERVE'S BOARD OF GOVERNORS have a special aura. So-called Fed watchers read profound meaning into every word the governors utter, and their actions are expected to change the course of history. On days when the Federal Reserve Board meets, business news broadcasts routinely lead with breathless pronouncements about the governors' latest statements and speculations about what they portend. The governors really should wear white robes and carry scepters to complete the picture. So Federal Reserve actions certainly must drive GDP cycles, no?

No. While the actions of the Fed certainly impact the investment world and are an important factor in your asset allocation decisions, they have nearly nothing (and I threw in the word "nearly" just to be polite) to do with GDP.

Do you doubt me, the Great and Powerful Gary? As usual, I ask that you peruse the pictures that drew me to my conclusion. They reflect the fact that the Federal Reserve attempts to influence the economy by adjusting any of three levers:

- The pace of money supply growth
- The amount of the assets held by the Fed
- The federal funds rate

Do the actions of the Fed in regard to these three levers have a measurable impact on the economy? Here's the data. First, Figure 7.4 tracks money supply growth compared with GDP growth. It brings back the M2 money supply measure I introduced in chapter two.

Figure 7.4. Money supply growth does not correlate with real GDP growth…(Sources: GDP—BEA. Inflation—BLS. Money supply—Federal Reserve.)

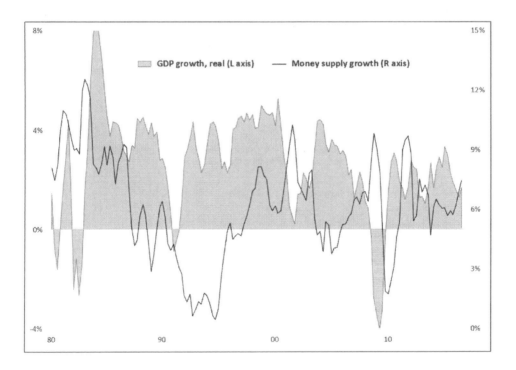

Over the last three and a half decades, the money supply has been gyrating all over the place, like a drunken infantryman (why always malign sailors?). But there is *no* direct correlation between the money supply and GDP growth. As I mentioned when discussing inflation in chapter four, the crucial link between the money supply and GDP is the velocity of money, which in turn is driven by banks' willingness to lend, which is part of the debt cycle. Tracing the money supply alone gives us no additional information that we can use to make our economic forecasting more accurate.

Okay, so the money supply is not a GDP driver. How about the volume of assets held by the Fed? To explain how the Fed's asset investment powers work, here's a bit of background. The Federal Reserve is allowed to own investments. If the Fed buys, say, a Treasury bond from a bank, it affects the financial markets in two ways. First, it creates more demand for those bonds, which (all else equal) lowers their interest rates. Second, it gives the owner of that bond cash in exchange, and banks can put that cash to work by lending it.

So let's see what kind of magic the Fed wizards can create by adjusting the amount of their asset holdings, relative to GDP (Figure 7.5).

Figure 7.5. Changes in the Federal Reserve's investment holdings do not appear to materially spur GDP growth. (Sources: GDP—BEA. Inflation—BLS. Money supply—Fed.)

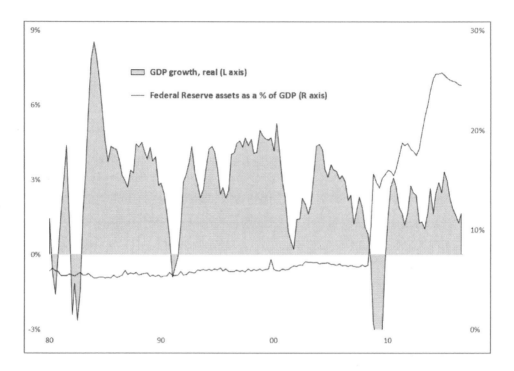

Not much to see here. The picture shows that the Fed has really used its asset buying powers only since 2008, in the wake of the financial crisis. The asset purchase program, which involved buying a massive $4 trillion of Treasury and mortgage-backed securities, was given the catchy name *quantitative easing* (QE). But Figure 7.5 shows no discernable link between QE and economic growth. The onset of QE was concurrent with a number of direct government actions that pulled the US out of the Great Recession, including massive government borrowing and the Troubled Asset Relief Program (TARP), which recapitalized the banking industry.

QE has since been employed not only by our Fed but by central banks in Europe, Japan, and the UK. As a result, bonds are far less attractive to own today. So QE has been important for your asset allocation decisions. But it is not a driver of economic growth.

I'll give the almighty Fed one last chance. Surely its control of short-term interest rates (see chapter three) must allow it to influence GDP growth. But Figure 7.6 reveals that, where there is any correlation at all between the federal funds rate and GDP growth, the fed funds rate *lags* GDP growth rather than drives it:

Figure 7.6. The fed funds rate lags GDP. (Sources: GDP—BEA. Inflation—BLS. Money supply—Fed.)

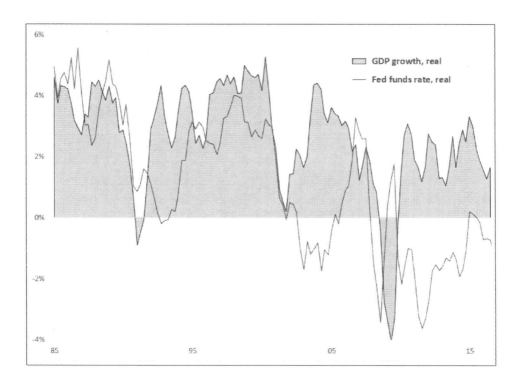

This seems counterintuitive. Shouldn't entities borrow more when interest rates are low? In which case, shouldn't interest rate changes drive debt growth rates, which in turn drive more GDP growth?

That makes logical sense, but reality doesn't follow the logic. To see why, let's test three big-ticket items that typically require significant debt financing: cars, houses, and business capital goods. First, let's look at car sales and interest rates.

Figure 7.7 compares new car sales with the average yield on a new car loan. Note that I inverted the car loan yield numbers because we are testing the proposition that lower interest rates means higher cars sales.

Figure 7.7. Changes in car loan rates don't have much at all to do with car sales. (Sources: New car sales—BEA. Car loan rates—Fed.)

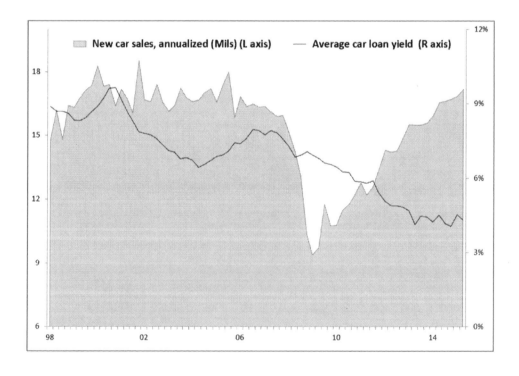

No correlation. Auto sales were roughly the same in 2017 with 4% loan rates as they were 15 years ago with double the loan rates. And car sales in 2001 with a 9% interest rate were the same as they were in 2004 at a 6% rate. So what *are* the (pun alert) key drivers of car sales? I identify two.

One is jobs. Statistical analysis tells us that year-over-year changes in employment explain 27% of the level of car sales, whereas changes in car loan rates explain only 6%. When you think about it, this makes all the sense in the world. Getting a job changes a family's income by many thousands of dollars a year. But a 1-percentage-point change in the interest rate on an $18,000, seven-year car loan changes the family's annual car payment by a mere $100 or so. It's obvious which factor will have a greater impact on a car buying decision.

Figure 7.8. Auto lender underwriting standards—in this case, LTV—have a major influence on car sales. (Sources: New car sales—BEA. Car loan-to-value ratio— Fed.)

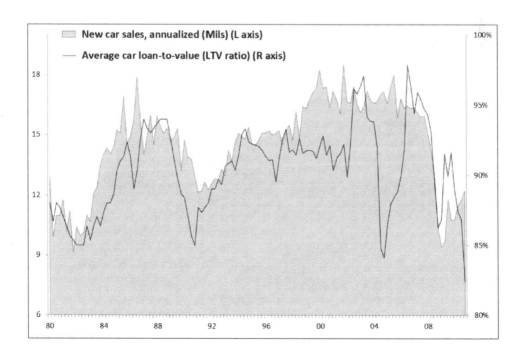

The second driver of new car sales is our old friend, lending standards. Check out Figure 7.8 (on the previous page), which compares car sales to the maximum allowable percentage of a car's value that lenders were willing to lend against (the loan-to-value, or LTV ratio). The correlation is pretty clear: The LTV explained 35% of the change in car sales.

Next, let's consider home sales and interest rates. The average mortgage used to buy a home is over $250,000 today. Common sense therefore suggests that the mortgage interest rate is critical to home sales. But the fact is that the relationship between interest rates and home sales is mixed.

Home sales are of two types: new homes and existing homes. I'll start by testing the correlation between mortgage rates and new home construction activity (Figure 7.9). Note that I again inverted the mortgage rate data to best visually test the theory that lower mortgage interest rates spur new home sales.

Figure 7.9. Home mortgage rates are largely irrelevant to home construction activity. (Sources: Housing starts—Census. Home mortgage rate—Fed.)

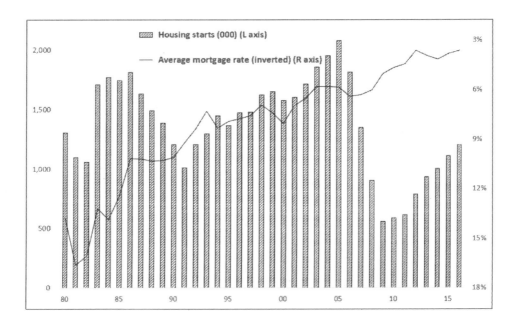

The theory turns out to be false. Some of the best housing start years occurred when mortgage rates were quite high, and recent record-low mortgage rates coincided with historically horrible building years. That statistical regression analysis I keep saying I'll never use says that changes in interest rates explain only 5% of the changes in housing starts.

Demographics are clearly the major factor in home construction activity over the long run. More young people forming households means more home construction demand. But in the shorter run, as I bet you can guess, the major influence is really home mortgage lending standards, which is another way of saying banks' willingness to lend (another appearance by our little buddy, the debt cycle!). The reason is that the biggest hurdle to homeownership for first-time buyers is the downpayment. When lenders are willing to accept smaller downpayments, more renters can become owners.

Figure 7.10 presents a snapshot of the 2000s housing bubble and bust. It compares home construction to the share of mortgage loans originated that didn't conform to Fannie Mae and Freddie Mac underwriting standards, namely subprime and other non-prime loans. More non-conforming loan volume is evidence of easier loan underwriting standards. And sure enough, home construction changes correlate well with mortgage lending standard changes.

Figure 7.10. The 2000s home construction boom and bust was largely a function of too-loose, then very tight home mortgage lending standards. (Sources: Housing starts—Census. Non-conforming loan share—Inside Mortgage Finance.)

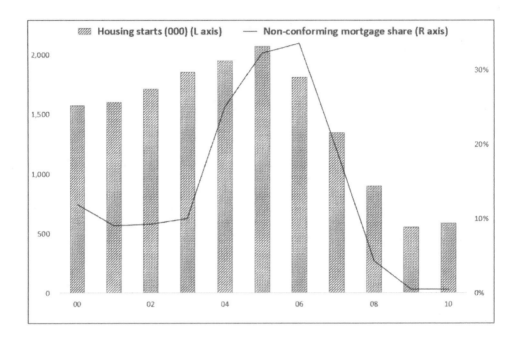

But mortgage interest rates *are* important to *existing* home sales, as Figure 7.11 shows. The graph shows housing turnover (existing home sales as a percentage of the whole housing stock) to reflect the fact that the housing stock, and therefore existing home sales, naturally grow over time. For clarity, I again inverted the mortgage rate data.

Figure 7.11. Unlike new home sales, the volume of existing home sales *is* materially influenced by interest rates. (Sources: Existing home sales—National Association of Realtors. Housing stock—Census. Mortgage rates—Freddie Mac.)

This time, the correlation is pretty good. Why? Because existing home-owners have more financial assets than the average new home buyer, including the equity already in their homes. Therefore, existing homeowners aren't as sensitive to changes in underwriting standards, and can be more sensitive to mortgage rates.

Finally, let's look at business equipment spending and interest rates. The cost of financing equipment purchases is very important to the purchase decision, or at least that's what they taught me, and I assume others, in business school. So there should be an important correlation between the two. But Figure 7.12 tells a largely different story.

Figure 7.12. Business equipment spending is only modestly correlated to interest rates. (Sources: Business equipment spending—BEA. Corporate bond yield—Moody's.)

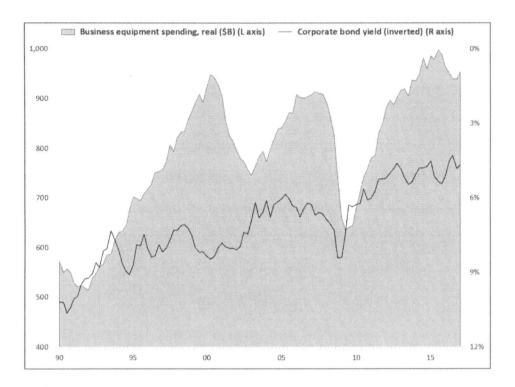

Why not a closer correlation? Because other variables are even more important to the business equipment purchase decision. One is return on investment. If a $200,000 robot can save me $500,000 in labor expenses over the next ten years, I'm buying the robot regardless of borrowing costs. And if my pizza place is only half full, I'm not buying another pizza oven no matter how low interest rates are.

In sum, the Federal Reserve does have a major influence on the yields we receive on cash and bonds, and therefore on our asset allocation decisions. But it has barely any impact on the debt cycle or the GDP cycle.

Consumer Income Doesn't Drive Economic Cycles

OKAY, WE'VE CONCLUDED THAT BUSINESSES and the Federal Reserve are followers of GDP growth, not leaders. But we live in a democracy, man. The citizen is king. The benefits of citizenship center largely around the freedom to buy stuff. Which means that consumers' income (DPI) and the choices consumers make about using that income must drive GDP. Let's test the relationship between DPI growth and GDP growth (Figure 7.13).

Figure 7.13. Changes in household income lag GDP changes. (Sources: GDP and consumer income—BEA. Inflation—BLS.)

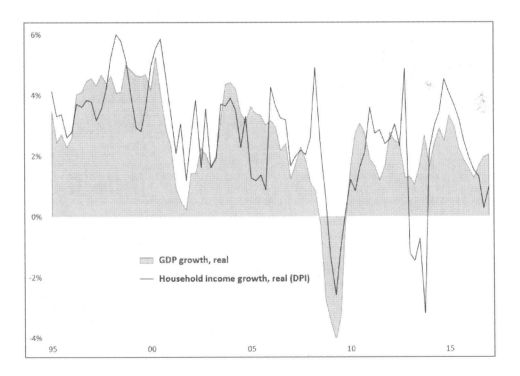

DPI growth *lags* GDP! How is that possible? Easy, if you keep in mind the theme of this book—debt. Consumers don't spend only their income as measured by DPI; they also spend borrowed money. Furthermore, consumers don't spend whatever portion of DPI they choose to save. Adjusting for consumer borrowing and savings links DPI with actual consumer spending as follows:

Consumer spending = Disposable income + borrowing – savings

Once this adjustment is made, we find that consumer spending correlates very closely to GDP, as you would logically expect (Figure 7.14).

Figure 7.14. Only actual consumer spending correlates with GDP. (Sources: GDP and consumer spending—BEA. Inflation—BLS.)

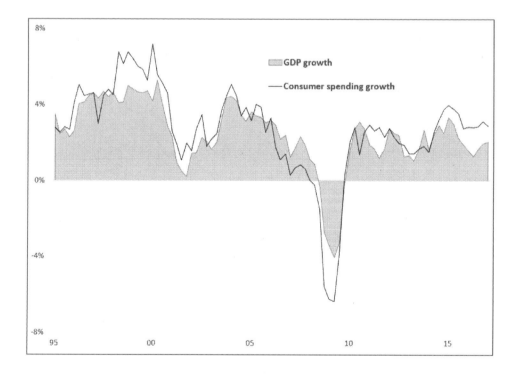

It is true that consumer spending cycles correlate with GDP cycles; after all, consumer spending accounts for roughly 70% of GDP, so the link between the two is inevitable. *But consumer borrowing and saving cycles drive consumer spending cycles.* So if you want to anticipate changes in GDP growth, and therefore changes in stock market performance, don't bother tracking personal income or consumer spending. Focus on changes in consumer borrowing and savings activity. They will tell you what you need to know.

Tax Rates Don't Drive Economic Cycles

ONE LAST FABLE TO DISPROVE. A common belief is that tax rates materially impact GDP growth. After all, you can spend only your *after*-tax income. So why work hard at your job—or, if you own a business, why launch a new product line—if Uncle Sam is just going to grab a big chunk of your cash?

Based on this reasoning, cutting taxes is often viewed as a way to juice GDP growth. For example, late in 2017, the US Treasury's Office of Tax Policy increased its forecast for GDP growth, stating, "Treasury expects approximately half of this 0.7% increase in GDP to come from changes in corporate taxation."

I bet by now you know what I plan to do with this argument. That's right, test it using real data. (By the way, the Treasury produced *no* data to support its forecast. Hmm.) I studied two types of tax rates: (1) the *top marginal tax rate* a person or business can pay on their top dollar of income, and (2) the *effective tax rate*, which is the percentage of all US taxes paid as a share of total income earned by businesses or individuals.

Figure 7.15 shows a history of business tax rates.

Figure 7.15. Business tax rates have steadily declined for the past 50 years, including both the top marginal rate and the effective tax rate. So it's hard to argue that business tax policy has contributed to slowing GDP growth (Sources: Tax rate—Census. Taxes paid—BEA. GDP—BEA. Inflation—BLS.)

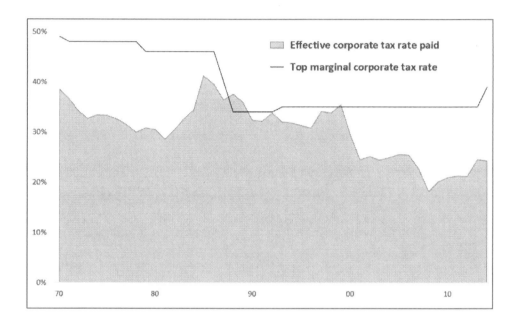

Both the effective and top marginal corporate tax rates have been in a general down trend over the past five decades. *And so has US GDP growth!* So lower business taxes show no tendency to increase GDP growth.

Further, many claims have been publicly made that the business tax cuts enacted in December, 2017, will spur business investment spending. Figure 7.16 shows that there is no correlation—repeat, *no* correlation—between tax rates and business investment spending.

Figure 7.16. Business tax rates have essentially nothing to do with the level of business investment spending. Customer demand is its primary driver.

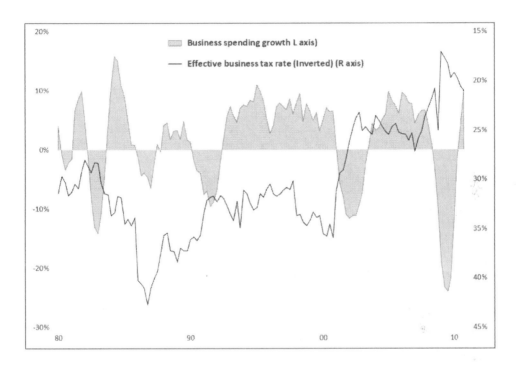

What actually does primarily drive business spending is changes in customer demand. Duh—businesses expand capacity when sales increases necessitate it. For example, here's a story from *The Wall Street Journal* about the steel industry, published on December 30, 2017, *after* the corporate tax cuts were enacted:

> Steelmakers are betting on the U.S. again, building mills they hope will help them compete against cheap imports as demand rises . . . Steel prices are also on the rise globally. And demand for U.S. steel is starting to rebound, thanks to rising oil prices and a strengthening manufacturing sector, steel executives say. They're also counting on additional U.S. tariffs to drive out cheap, foreign-made steel . . . Stiff tariffs imposed over the past 18 months have

significantly slowed steel imports from China, according to Commerce Department reports.

Lots on steel demand and supply. Not a single mention in the article about the tax cut.

What about personal income tax rates? Figure 7.17 shows a history of the top marginal and effective tax rates for all US individuals.

Figure 7.17. The effective individual tax rate has been quite stable over a long time, while the top marginal rate has bounced around. (Sources: Tax rate—Census. Taxes paid—BEA. GDP—BEA. Inflation—BLS.)

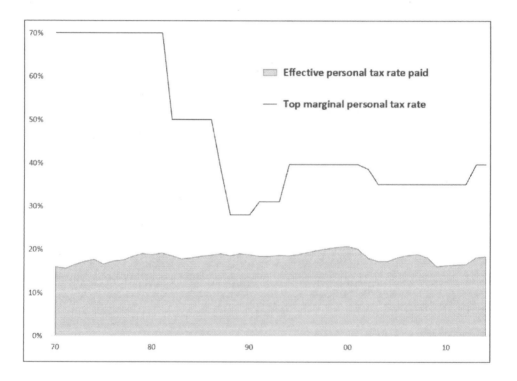

The chart shows that, while the top marginal tax rate has varied significantly, the percentage of our aggregate income that we pay in taxes has been remarkably stable, even as GDP growth rates have fluctuated. So the *effective* individual tax rate clearly has nothing to do with GDP growth. I am therefore left with only one tax rate that can possibly influence GDP growth—the top marginal personal tax rate.

Before you look at Figure 7.18 (no peeking, I'm serious), two points to note. First, I use a different time measure for GDP growth here than my usual annual rate of increase. I compare the tax rate to the average change in GDP growth over the following three years, assuming that people need some time to adjust their economic behavior to a new tax rate. Second, I *invert* the depiction of the tax rate, putting lower rates at the top of the graph and higher rates at the bottom, based on the obvious assumption that the lower the tax rate, the higher GDP growth should be going forward.

Now you're allowed to view Figure 7.18.

Figure 7.18. Tax cuts in the early 1980s and the early 2000s both coincided with better GDP growth. Does that prove a correlation? (Sources: Tax rate—Census. GDP—BEA. Inflation—BLS.)

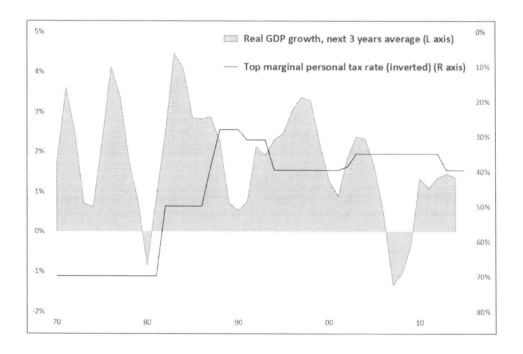

Maybe we have something here. The large tax cut in 1982 coincided with strong GDP growth, as did the much smaller 2003 tax cut. But the large 1987 tax cut coincided with *slowing* GDP growth. What gives?

The explanation is that *tax rate changes influence GDP in two ways.* I've already noted that tax rate changes are assumed to impact the *willingness* of people to work and of businesses to invest. But tax rate changes also impact *basic cash flow.* A couple of simple examples will explain what I mean.

First, assume the following simple government budget: Moe gets $30,000 a year in Social Security payments, and Larry pays $30,000 in taxes. So the government is even. Now the government gives Larry a $5,000 tax cut. Moe still receives—and spends—his $30,000 in Social Security benefits. But now Larry's tax bill is only $25,000, so he has an extra $5,000 to spend— but at the cost of requiring the government to borrow $5,000.

For a second example, assume that Curly made $50,000 last year and spent it all. This year, Curly made the same $50,000, but spent $55,000 by running up a $5,000 credit card bill. Now Curly has an extra $5,000 to spend—at the cost of borrowing $5,000.

In both examples, there is more GDP per person in the second year. But neither Moe, Larry, nor Curly worked any harder; they just borrowed more.

It turns out that the same basic process occurred in the real world of the tax cuts of 1982, 1987, and 2003. Table 7.1 shows the changes in total debt growth in the three years before and after the tax cuts.

Table 7.1. The tax cuts of 1982 and 2003 coincided with sharp increases in debt growth, so it is unclear whether the tax cuts contributed much at all to GDP growth. (Source: Fed.)

Tax cut of:			Three year total debt growth ($ billions)			Total change in debt growth, after versus before
			Federal government borrowing	Private sector borrowing	Total borrowing	
1982	Before	'79-'81	$226	$871	$1,096	
	After	'82-'84	589	1,113	1,701	+$605
1987	Before	'84-'86	$727	$1,703	$2,429	
	After	'87-'89	543	1,539	2,082	($347)
2003	Before	'00-'02	$62	$2,994	$3,056	
	After	'03-'05	1,157	4,501	5,659	+$2,603

This table shows why the tax cuts of 1982 and 2003 seemed to generate a bigger GDP boost than the cut of 1987: far more total debt growth accompanied them. The 1982 and 2003 cuts were part of an economic package that included a rise in military spending and financial system deregulation, which supported booms in private-sector borrowing. In fact, I'd argue that the debt growth created by the tax cuts and especially by the added private sector borrowing was far more important than any tax incentives in creating the GDP increases of 1982 and 2003.

Finally, let's apply some common sense to the tax-rate discussion. A popular belief is that high tax rates, particularly capital gains tax rates, inhibit entrepreneurship. I doubt it, unless the tax rates are well over 50%. For example, consider the movie *The Social Network*, which tells the story of the founding of Facebook. Remember the scene where Mark Zuckerberg nearly stops working on the Facebook app after he learns that he will have to pay a capital gains tax if he is successful?

No, neither do I, because there was no discussion of tax rates in the movie. Nor was there much discussion of the topic in the pizza-box-strewn offices of Facebook, I'll bet.

Tax rates alone simply don't drive entrepreneurs. What does? Marcus Ryu, co-founder and CEO of Guidewire Software, answered this question in a *New York Times* op-ed piece (October 9, 2017):

> As an entrepreneur myself and a friend to many others, I know that lower tax rates will not motivate people to start companies. People start companies for many reasons: a compelling idea, ambition for fame or fortune, a desire to be one's own boss, frustration with one's employer. I have never heard someone say, "I would have started a company, but tax rates were too high" or "I wouldn't have started this company, but then George W. Bush cut tax rates, so I did."

This guy must know what he's talking about. He took his company public in 2012 at $13 per share. Its price in mid-June of 2018 was $92.

By the same token, people always want to make more money, whether they can keep 70% of it or 50% of it. Would some people possibly give less effort if they could keep only 10%? Sure. But I doubt whether the difference between a 40% maximum tax rate and a 38% rate changes anyone's actual behavior.

Finally, remember that some or most of the extra earnings from lower tax rates will be saved, not spent. To that extent, a lower tax rate doesn't help GDP. We actually have evidence that that this is true following the 2018 personal tax cut. Taxes paid were reduced by about $300 billion annualized through April, and savings increased by a similar amount. That is especially true when it comes to tax changes to the wealthy. Bill Gates isn't waiting for a tax cut to finally get those Kevin Durant sneakers he has been coveting. If you want to get technical—and who doesn't?—this behavior is called the *marginal propensity to consume*. The more you earn, the less likely you are to spend the next dollar of income.

Despite all of this evidence, many influential people continue to believe the theory that tax policy is a key economic driver. Here's a great theory mistake made by Lawrence Kudlow, the current (as of this writing; jobs change quickly in Washington these days) US Chief Economic Advisor, from a book called *Superforecasting* by Philip Tetlock and Dan Gardner:

> Kudlow's one Big Idea is supply-side economics. When President George W. Bush followed the supply-side prescription by enacting substantial tax cuts, Kudlow was certain an economic boom of equal magnitude would follow . . . Reality fell short: growth and job creation were positive but somewhat disappointing relative to the long-term average . . . In December 2007, months after the first rumblings of the financial crisis had been felt, . . . Kudlow was optimistic. "There is no recession," he wrote. "In fact we are about to enter the seventh consecutive year of the Bush boom." *In fact*, of course, what followed was the Great Recession.

Kudlow's punishment for being wrong? A lucrative career since as a CNBC talking head followed by an appointment as one of the Trump administration's key financial advisors. A flawed but tempting theory (something for nothing) trumps reality yet again.

The silver lining is that we investors can take advantage of this craziness, as I discuss in chapter nine.

8   The Great Modernization:
How Debt Became the Key Driver of US Economic and Investment Cycles

HOPEFULLY BY NOW the importance of the debt cycle in understanding economic and investment cycles is crystal clear. But why has the debt cycle become so important?

A key reason is that, since 1980, debt itself has become a much larger part of the US economy, as illustrated in Figure 8.1.

Figure 8.1. Debt growth began playing a greater role in the US economy in about 1980. (Sources: GDP—BEA. Debt—Fed.)

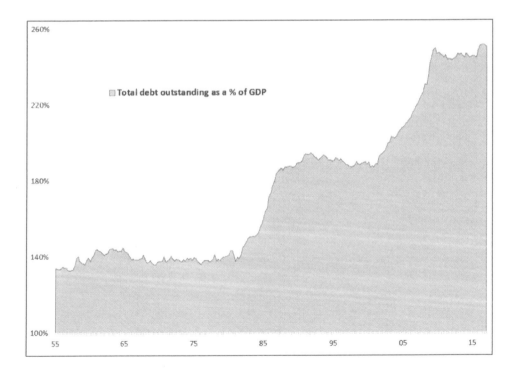

Why the drastic change in debt levels following 1980? I am convinced it was a reaction to the steadily declining GDP growth rate that began in the 1970s.

Figure 8.2 shows an eight-year average growth rate for GDP. I use eight years because that has been the average time between recessions since the 1950s. Therefore, the eight-year average tends to smooth out the ebbs and flows of the normal economic cycle, emphasizing instead the long-term trend—what economists call the *secular* trend. The picture shows the slowing growth rate of GDP over the course of the 1970s, several decades of stability at a lower growth rate, then another material leg down over the past 15 years.

Figure 8.2. I believe that the sharp rise in debt outstanding since 1980 was a reaction to the secular decline in GDP growth that began during the 1970s. Sources: GDP—BEA. Inflation rate—BLS.)

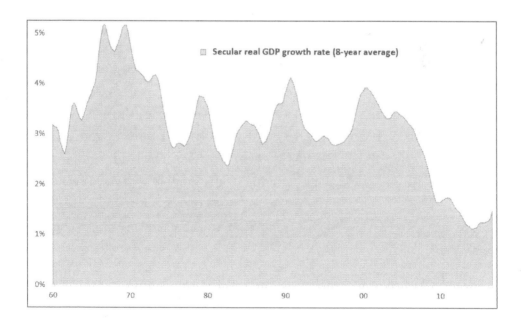

As usual, the answer to one question elicits more questions. Why the secular decline in GDP? "Secular decline" sounds bad, as if the US has failed in some way. But don't feel guilty. It's not your fault. I view the GDP decline as the result of natural economic trends. Those trends include:

- Slowing population growth
- Increased economic competition, from Europe and especially Asia
- Declining labor productivity growth due to the shift from a manufacturing economy to a service economy
- Increased government regulation to achieve non-economic goals

These four trends collectively constitute what I call the *Great Modernization*. Let's dig deeper. Mental shovels ready, dear reader.

Slowing Population Growth

A FEW YEARS BACK, IT WAS FASHIONABLE to talk about "job creators," usually identified as entrepreneurs, business people, or just rich people in general. With all due respect to the wealthy, evidence suggests that the primary creators of jobs—and of GDP growth—not only in the US but everywhere on Earth, are moms. Remember that GDP is gross domestic *product*, so each new human being adds to the demand for products (and services)—more diapers and strollers at first, then eventually more kale, more sweatpants, more pedicures, more smartphone covers, and so on. So the more babies, the more GDP.

This common-sense insight is backed up by data. Figure 8.3 compares long-term GDP growth with long-term US population growth.

Figure 8.3. The secular decline in GDP was partly caused by slowing population growth. (Source: BEA.)

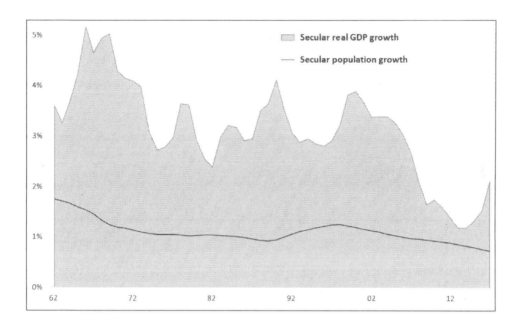

The picture suggests some relationship between the two. The fact that annual population growth slowed considerably over the past 60 years— from 1.5% down to 0.8% —explains a lot of the slowdown in GDP growth since the 1970s.

Working backward, two big factors influenced the rate of US population growth over the past four decades. The negative influence was a sharp decline in the birth rate. Figure 8.4 shows that the US birth rate, measured as the number of births per 1,000 population, declined sharply from the Baby Boom of the mid-1950s into the early 1970s, then started another slow decline beginning about 1990. Lots of social factors have gone into this decline, which I'll leave to others to explain.

Figure 8.4. The US population growth rate has been declining primarily because the birth rate has fallen sharply. (Sources: Population—BEA. Births—National Vital Statistics Reports, US Department of Health and Human Services.)

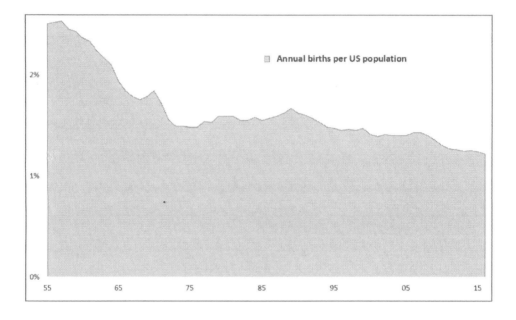

The positive influence on population growth was a rise in immigration. The US Citizenship and Immigration Services estimates that net immigration increased from three million during the 1960s to seven million during the 1980s to 11 million during the 2000s. And the Migration Policy Institute estimates that the number of Americans who are immigrants rose from 10 million in 1960 to 43 million in 2015. But this increased immigration only partially compensated for the birth rate decline.

One economic sector that clearly shows the link between slower population growth and slower GDP growth is real estate construction. The fewer new people added, the fewer new homes, stores, offices, and other forms of infrastructure that are logically needed. And sure enough, as the growth of the US population has slowed, so has the value of total residential and commercial real estate construction as a share of GDP, as Figure 8.5 shows.

Figure 8.5. Real estate construction is a clear victim of slowing population growth. (Source: BEA.)

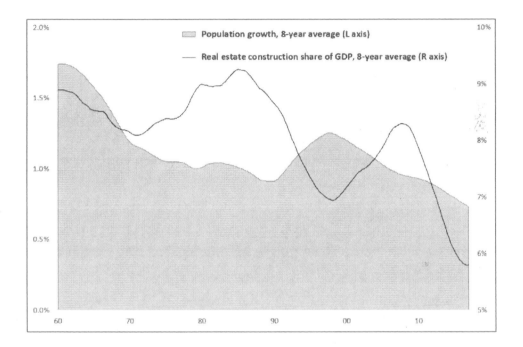

Increasing Economic Competition

THE SECOND CAUSE of slowing GDP growth in the US was the return of economic competition from abroad.

Let's start by traveling back in time to 1945. As the artillery smoke clears away from the concluding battles of World War II, we see the industrial might of Germany, France, England, Japan, and many other countries lying in ruins. The social and political infrastructure of these societies has also been shattered. In fact, instability will rage for another decade or more in both Europe and Asia, with the onset of the Cold War, political crises in Berlin and Hungary, wars in Korea and Vietnam, revolution in China, and much more. Throughout this period, the US stands nearly alone as a great industrial power, giving us a huge economic advantage over the rest of the world. If we built it, they had to buy it. Hence our large positive trade balance throughout the 1950s and 1960s.

But by the 1970s, Europe, Japan, and South Korea had made big strides to rebuild their industrial bases and become effective economic competitors to the US.

Further, in 1960, a number of oil-producing countries formed a cartel called the Organization of the Petroleum Exporting Countries (OPEC). During the 1970s, the OPEC countries, initially for political reasons, coordinated to sharply increase the price of oil, to their economic benefit and the US's detriment.

Finally, the 1990s brought the advent of China as a powerful low-cost industrial competitor. Other Asian countries followed, like Indonesia and Vietnam, as well as non-Asian countries like Mexico. These new competitors to the US have made inroads largely because of their much lower wages. For example, while the average US assembly line worker today makes $16 an hour, his or her competitor in Mexico makes only about $3 an hour. Manufacturing companies seeking sites for expansion have long taken note.

All of this new competition led to an inevitable decline in the US trade balance (Figure 8.6).

Figure 8.6. US post-World War II economic dominance began to erode during the 1970s as Europe recovered and Asia industrialized. The changes can be seen in the history of the US trade balance. Sources: GDP and trade balance—BEA. Inflation—BLS.)

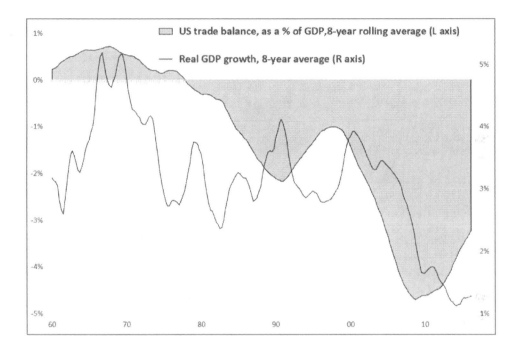

Since a trade deficit subtracts from GDP, a rising deficit logically puts downward pressure on GDP.

Declining Productivity Growth

GDP GROWTH CAN BE BROKEN INTO TWO COMPONENTS: population growth and growth in the amount of GDP produced per person. Another term for "GDP produced per person" is *labor productivity*. Figure 8.7 shows a history of labor productivity growth in the US.

Figure 8.7. A history of US labor productivity growth, defined as GDP produced per person. (Sources: GDP and population growth—BEA. Inflation rate—BLS.)

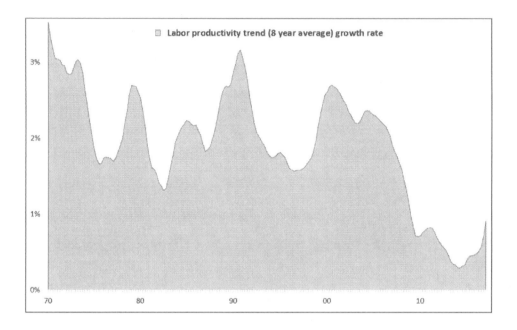

Note the steady decline in productivity growth since a 1990 peak. Why?

Labor productivity is driven by lots of factors. Analyzing it—and figuring out how to increase it—occupies the time of scores of earnest economists and many equally earnest but better-paid business executives. I'll focus on just one very important productivity driver here: the huge shift in the makeup of America's labor force. To explain, I'll break the labor force into three buckets—manufacturing, private-sector services, and government services.

Figure 8.8 shows that the relative size of these three buckets has shifted dramatically. Since 1952, manufacturing's share of American employment steadily declined. Beginning around 1970, private-sector service jobs took off, and their share of the economy has continued to grow ever since. Contrary to popular belief, the share represented by government services has not skyrocketed in recent decades but rather has remained about the same.

Figure 8.8. The share growth of service jobs and the decline in manufacturing job share has slowed US productivity growth. (Source: US Department of Labor.)

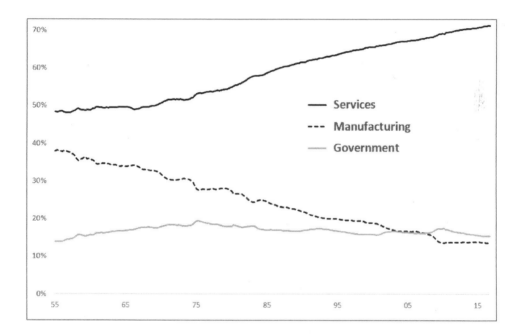

The impact of the shifting labor buckets on US productivity is pretty clear. Labor productivity growth peaked right around the time when the service sector share started rising, and has slowly declined ever since. That's not a coincidence. Service businesses have historically had a much harder time generating productivity gains than manufacturers. Yes, technology has made many service jobs redundant—there are fewer secretaries, travel agents, and bank tellers working today than in the past. But technology can't reduce the number of people needed to provide a massage from one to less than one. And in major fields like medicine, education, and law, technology has made scarcely any inroads into the employment numbers (at least so far). So service businesses tend to enjoy lower rates of productivity growth than manufacturing businesses.

The numbers tell the tale. I calculate that since 1960, manufacturing productivity in the US grew by an average of 3.0% per year. Meanwhile, services sector productivity improved by only 1.3% annually. I estimate that the shift towards a more service-based economy since 1960 has cost the US about 0.4% a year in productivity improvement, and therefore subtracted the same amount from GDP growth.

Increased Government Regulation

A FOURTH MAJOR DRAG ON GDP GROWTH has been increased government regulation to achieve non-economic goals.

Regulations are rules of behavior. It seems logical that the more rules the government imposes on economic behavior, the more challenging it will be for businesses to thrive. And in fact the volume of new regulations correlates pretty darn well with the slowdown in productivity growth the US has experienced over the past four decades, as Figure 8.9 shows

Note that my measure of government regulatory behavior is the number of pages added to the Federal Register each year—an admittedly inexact metric for activity that is highly diverse and therefore quite complicated to measure precisely. But the picture jibes with the common-sense observation that government regulation has steadily increased over the years.

Figure 8.9. Increased government regulation has also slowed productivity. (Sources: Productivity based on GDP and population—BEA. Inflation—BLS. Regulatory pages published—Federal Register.)

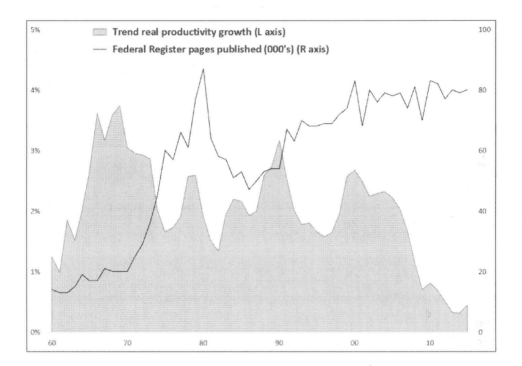

What's behind the increase in regulations? Who would want to slow productivity, and therefore hamper GDP growth? Conspiracy theorists point to power-hungry bureaucrats as the villains. But I believe the story is more fundamental than that. The drive to create orderly systems of social cooperation is built into our DNA.

Consider, for example, this passage from science writer Ed Yong's best-selling book *I Contain Multitudes: The Microbes Within Us and a Grander View of Life* (Ecco, 2016):

> Every major transition in the history of life—from single-celled to multi-celled, from individuals to symbiotic collectives—has had to solve the same

problem: how can the selfish interests of individuals be overcome to form cooperative groups?

So in a sense, the need for regulation started with one-celled creatures. It poses a challenging dilemma for every form of life—including humans, as Yong observes:

> H.G. Wells wrote about this in 1930: "Every symbiosis is, in some degree, underlain with hostility, and only by proper regulation and often elaborate adjustment can the state of mutual benefit be maintained. Even in human affairs, the partnerships for mutual benefit are not so easily kept up . . . "

The creation of rules, norms, and systems—in other words, regulation—is necessary to maintain a civil and well-functioning society. The more people there are in the world, the greater the opportunities for someone to tee us off and complicate things. And the more technology, the greater the complexity of our economic and social lives. If you doubt me, check out Facebook's recent privacy travails. More complications require regulators to negotiate more compromises—or declare more winners—among the various competing interests in the population.

Note that regulation is not always an economic downer; it can also increase GDP. For example, setting common business practice standards across the country helps companies expand without having to deal with a myriad of state laws. Anti-trust legislation fights company efforts to stifle competition and innovation. Legislation to build infrastructure to promote business activities, from railroads in the 1800s to highways in the 1950s clearly increased GDP over the long term. So did a lot of government-funded scientific research in healthcare, technology, the space program, and so on.

I also believe that when national wealth increases, it naturally spurs more regulation. Most of us agree that having more money is better. But as our incomes increase, getting even more money declines on our list of desires. Is Lebron James excitedly looking forward to the next payment from his shoe endorsement deal, which *Sports Illustrated* estimates to be worth over $1 billion over its life? Probably not as much as the average citizen looks forward to winning $1,000 on a scratch-off lottery ticket. Once our wealth reaches a certain level, other goals tend to become more urgent—personal satisfaction, economic fairness, a healthy environment, and social justice.

We see this happening not just on an individual level but also on a society-wide level. For example, when China was poorer, its citizens were willing to accept pollution, workplace injuries, counterfeit goods, draconian limits on family size, rampant government corruption, and other serious social ills in exchange for faster economic growth. But as the Chinese population has gotten more affluent, its priorities are shifting, as this quotation from *The Wall Street Journal* (December 26, 2017) indicates:

> China is adopting a new green index in a bid to pressure local governments to reduce pollution . . . The indicator is meant to guide local governments on development and send a signal to focus less on rapid growth at the expense of the environment.

If you're still inclined to dismiss all regulation as a needless imposition on personal freedom, consider what libertarian football would be like. If the sport had no rules, then every time a pass receiver tried to get open for a pass, a defender would tackle him long before the quarterback could launch his throw. That wouldn't make for an interesting game. That's why rules have been created to protect the receiver's ability to run downfield.

Furthermore, football rules have evolved over time as the tactics of the receivers and defenders have changed. Referees have to make constant judgment calls about whether the rules have been broken on any individual play—and we fans then criticize the referees, especially when our team gets the short end of the stick. But this messy mixture of evolving rules and imperfect enforcement still makes for a more entertaining game than having no rules at all.

Personal Financial Engineering—
A Consequence of the Great Modernization

AS YOU MIGHT EXPECT, US WAGE GROWTH benefited enormously from the economic booms of the 1950s and 1960s. It then suffered as GDP growth subsequently slowed (Figure 8.10).

Figure 8.10. Wage growth naturally slowed with the secular slowdown in GDP, which didn't make wage earners happy. (Sources: Wages—BEA. Inflation—BLS.)

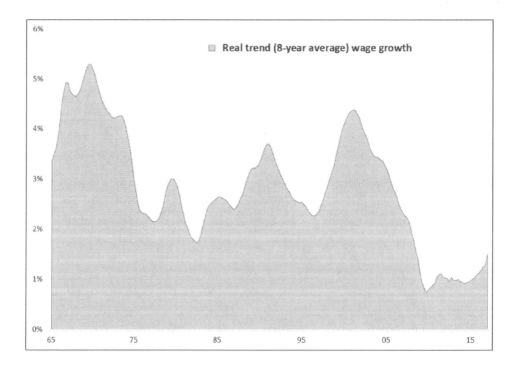

Slowing wage growth suggests slowing spending growth. But we Americans are made of sterner stuff. The average American household is not about to let a mere wage slowdown cut into its spending growth. Since 1980, real US household spending grew one half of one percent faster annually than real household income. While that doesn't sound like much, the cumulative difference is significant. By 2017, instead of real household spending being 235% greater than in 1980, the extra spending made it 280% greater.

How did we Americans magically maintain faster spending growth than wage growth for the past four decades? Through *personal financial engineering*. Wall Street wizards have nothing on John and Jane Doe.

Personal financial engineering takes two forms. One is *increased borrowing*. As the Great Modernization took hold in the early 1980s, US households increased the rate at which they supplemented their spending through borrowing, as Figure 8.11 shows.

Figure 8.11. Since the 1980s, US households have been borrowing more . . .
(Sources: Borrowing—Fed. GDP—BEA.)

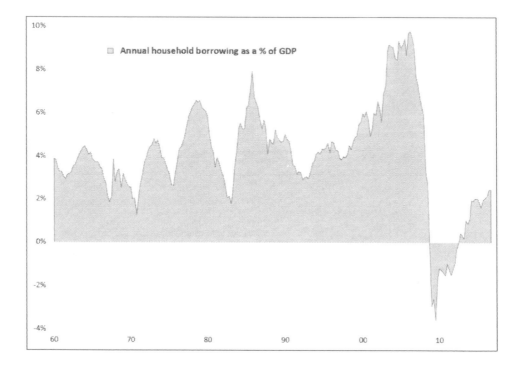

The other half of personal financial engineering is declining *financial savings*. Financial savings refers to the net amount of money we put in our savings and investment funds—bank and brokerage accounts, mutual funds, pension plans, and so on. Note that the BEA reports a monthly savings rate based on a definition different from my own, but the trends are similar. Figure 8.12 is a history of US household financial savings as a percentage of GDP.

Figure 8.12. . . . And saving less. (Sources: Financial savings—BEA and Fed. GDP—BEA.)

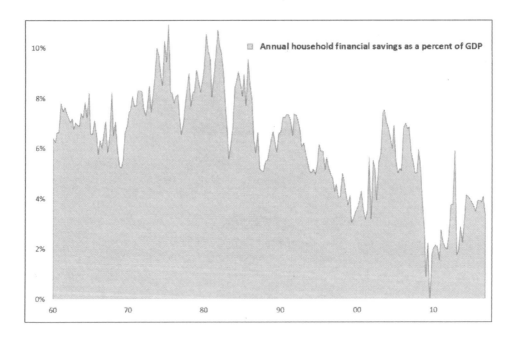

Figure 8.12 shows that the savings rate steadily declined since the late 1970s. Part of the reason is the slowdown in wages I discussed above; when shrinking discretionary income forced people to choose between putting something aside for retirement or nabbing that Sony Walkman, iPod, or Samsung Galaxy S9, guess which won out? But the declining savings rate

was also due to good news, namely the "wealth effect." If the value of your investments is rising nicely on its own, why add more out of your paycheck? Figure 8.13 shows that a huge rise in net worth relative to income since 1980 paved the way for a lower savings rate (inverted here):

Figure 8.13. The wealth effect. The greater our financial assets relative to our income, the less we save, and the more we spend. (Sources: Financial savings— BEA and Fed. Net worth to income—Fed.)

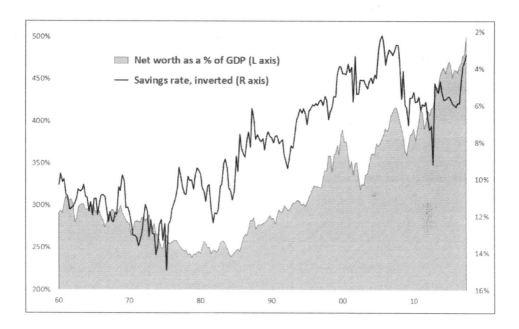

Before 1981, net saving and borrowing reduced US consumer spending by 4% of GDP; the combination reduced GDP because households saved more money than they borrowed. Since 1981, the average dropped to 1% of GDP—a little like a 3% pay raise without having to do any more work. But in 2007, the annoying truth that "There's no such thing as a free lunch" kicked in, and the consequences of overborrowing for 25 years showed up in the form of a wave of mortgage defaults and credit card charge-offs.

Furthermore, the same combination of trends has left more households nearing retirement with inadequate savings. As a result, increasing our spending through personal financial engineering has gotten more challenging.

Where oh where could another free lunch be found? Let me think. I've got it—Uncle Sam! It's nice to have an uncle in the money-printing business.

The free lunch derives from a dramatic shift in *net government transfer payments*. Huh? Let me explain. We US citizens *receive* cash from the government in the form of Social Security checks, subsidized health care through Medicare and Medicaid, disability payments, food stamps, unemployment insurance, and so on. We US citizens also *pay* cash to the government in the form of income and payroll taxes. *Net* government transfer payments are what you get when you add up our benefits and subtract our taxes.

Figure 8.14 shows how these payments have varied over the past 50+ years, calculated as a percentage of disposable personal income (DPI).

Figure 8.14. The new free lunch: net government transfer payments. They have replaced more consumer borrowing and less savings as a source of extra spending power. (Source: BEA.)

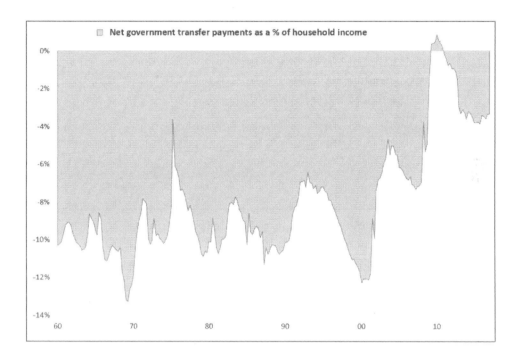

Why are the net government transfer payments shown in Figure 8-14 nearly always negative? To understand why, think of the government as having two basic functions. One is providing services, like the military, infrastructure, diplomacy, and regulations. The other function is income transfers—from middle-aged workers to retirees, from the wealthy to the poor, and from the healthy to the sick. As a nation, our tax payments cover both government functions. Table 8.1 offers a summary of these functions as reflected in the federal budget.

Table 8.1. US federal government budget results for 2017, broken out by services and income transfers (in $ millions).

U.S. federal government budget, 2017 ($ billions)	
Household income and estate taxes	$1,587
Business income and other taxes	567
Total income and other taxes	**$2,154**
Social Security	(888)
Medicare	(591)
Payroll Taxes	1,162
Net retirement programs	**($317)**
Medicaid	(439)
Other net benefit programs	(542)
Other government transfer payments	**($981)**
Government transfer expenses	**($1,298)**
Net tax collections after transfers	**$856**
Defense	(590)
Nondefense	(669)
Net interest	(263)
Government services expenses	**($1,522)**
Net government deficit	**($666)**

Our tax payments covered transfer payments with $856 billion left over to pay for government services. But the cost of services was $ 1.5 trillion, leaving a $666 billion shortfall that had to be covered with borrowing.

In 1960, the average cost of net transfer payments was around 10% of disposable income. But over the succeeding decades, as if by magic, the net transfer cost dropped dramatically, to only about 3% today—just as US households lost the ability to supplement their income with borrowed money. Voila! Free lunch—or, more precisely, a much cheaper lunch than our parents enjoyed. The hidden cost of the free lunch is, of course, more debt—in this case, government debt.

Political support for debt-driven free lunches is bipartisan. In the left corner, wearing blue trunks and fighting against the "deficit scolds," we have the liberal economist and columnist Paul Krugman. In a *New York Times* article from August 21, 2015, Krugman wrote:

> There's a reasonable argument to be made that part of what ails the world economy right now is that governments aren't deep enough in debt...The power of the deficit scolds was always a triumph of ideology over evidence . . . Issuing debt is a way to pay for useful things, and we should do more of that when the price is right.

In the right corner, wearing red trunks and fighting for all those who love lower taxes, is *National Review* magazine's take on the Republican Party at present:

> The CBO now expects the national debt to reach $30 trillion by 2027 and to double as a share of the national economy by mid century. Debt of such enormous proportions will have very real economic consequences . . . Yet, as we sink deeper and deeper into this ocean of red ink, both congressional Republicans and the Trump administration seem blithely unconcerned . . . OMB director Mick Mulvaney confessed that, despite warnings about the debt, President Trump remains stubbornly opposed to any attempts to reform entitlement programs such as Social Security or Medicare.

If the general population likes debt growth, and thought leaders of many persuasions like it, and politicians generally favor it, it's not a stretch to say that there is a general bias towards growing debt whenever possible.

Under the circumstances, it's not surprising that debt growth has come to be a major driver of US economic growth . . . and that the debt cycle has become a very important factor for you to be aware of as a savvy investor.

We Are Not Alone

THE US IS FAR FROM BEING THE ONLY country that has adopted debt growth as a temporary form of economic growth. Hoping to get something for nothing is not a national foible but a human trait, as Figure 8.15 shows:

Figure 8.15. Using debt to increase spending power is universal behavior, not just an American thing, as these historical ratios of total debt to GDP show. (Source: Bank for International Settlements.)

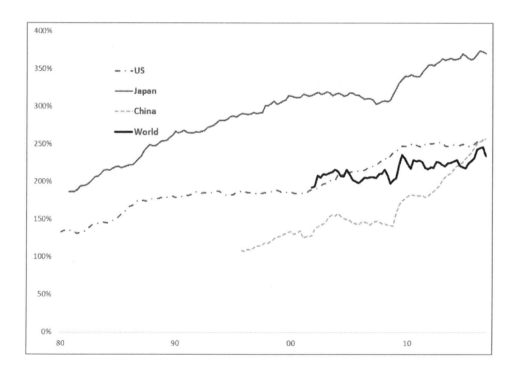

Figure 8.15 teaches us a few very important truths.

Financial leverage—that is, the level of debt—has been steadily increasing across the globe. If racking up high levels of debt is a sin, then we Americans are far from the only sinners. US financial leverage is actually only at the global average, and has been for the past two decades. Of course, the US has a lot to do with setting the global average, since its $47 trillion of debt at the end of 2016 represented 29% of the $160 trillion total of global debt. (I wonder: How does the debt held by planet Earth stack up against other planets in the universe? Are there highly leveraged countries on Mercury and Saturn? Note to self: Movie idea—*The Debt Bubble from Outer Space*. Call agent.)

Japan is today's global debt king, at nearly 400% total debt to equity. Japan had a decades-long private sector debt boom, which took its household and business debt from 116% of GDP in 1965 to 220% in 1994. This far exceeded the US record of 169% at the peak of our housing bubble. Japan's private sector has deleveraged ever since, a process that has, remarkably, continued for over three decades. But as in the US, the government stepped in to offset the private sector deleveraging. And when I say offset . . . wow! When private sector debt leverage peaked in 1994, government debt was 62% of Japan's GDP. At the end of 2016, it was 213%. By comparison, profligate Italy is only at 133%, and even bankrupt Greece (yes, I said it) is only at 179%.

China is the future debt king. Figure 8.15 shows the incredible speed at which China has leveraged over the past decade. Japan and the US never approached that pace of growth. It is very hard to imagine that China can avoid a financial crisis like the one experienced by every other country with a similar debt bubble.

Financial leverage can't rise indefinitely. GDP growth increases during the phase when debt expands, but it stops or reverses when the leveraging inevitably pauses, as happened in the US after the bursting of the debt bubbles of the 1980s and the 2000s. Greece, Spain, and Ireland suffered actual economic depressions when their mid-2000s bubbles ended.

෨

Perhaps you are hooked on phonics. Others are hooked on a feeling (either the B.J. Thomas original or the Blue Swede cover, which bizarrely added the line "Ooga-chaka Ooga-Ooga"). Others are hooked on prescription medicines. America's economy? Hooked on debt. I described in this chapter our felt need for it to juice our disappointing economic growth. The debt boom/bust cycles have in turn been major drivers of investment performance.

That makes it all the more important for investors to pay close attention to the debt cycle when making asset allocation decisions. In the next chapter, I'll spell out my forecast for the debt cycle and its implications for your investment decisions over the next three years.

9   Applying What You've Learned: An Asset Allocation Plan for Today

NOW IT'S TIME TO USE WHAT WE'VE LEARNED to estimate today's four investment variables that drive my earnings yield valuation model:

- The time value of money
- Inflation
- Earnings growth
- Market risk

Forecasting changes in these variables allows us to determine whether the 1-year CD, the 10-year Treasury bond, and the S&P 500 stock index are currently relatively cheap or expensive. We then use this knowledge to adjust our asset allocation accordingly. The forecasts I offer in this chapter look three years out to 2021, a suitable timeframe for asset allocation decisions.

First up, the time value of money. Excited? Me too.

My Time Value of Money Forecast: Reverting Towards the Mean

RECALL THAT THE TIME VALUE OF MONEY is the after-inflation return on investment that investors expect for tying up their money. In chapter four, I estimated that the historical average time value of money for the 1-year CD is 1.5% and for the 10-year Treasury bond is 2.5%.

In actuality, however, in mid-2018 the time value for the average bank 1-year CD rate was not positive 1.5% but 0%. The average 1-year CD interest rate banks were paying in mid-2018 was 0.4%, but banks are currently offering 0.7% on average and some online banks are paying 2.0%. I'll assume you are resourceful and can earn that 2.0% on your marginal cash investment. With inflation currently also running at about 2.0%, I calculate the short-term time value as 0%.

As I've explained, both the 1-year CD rate and the 10-year Treasury bond rate are very largely determined by the Federal Reserve through its setting of the fed funds rate. So to forecast the future time value of money, we have to forecast Federal Reserve monetary policy. We must start with why its recent policy has been so unusual. I believe the answer lies in Figure 9.1, which tracks the ratio of total debt out-standing to GDP.

Figure 9.1. Since 2002, the Federal Reserve has aided and abetted the surge in the US debt burden by lowering real debt costs. It is unlikely to change this policy significantly going forward. (Sources: Debt data and fed funds rate—Fed. GDP—BEA. Inflation—BLS.)

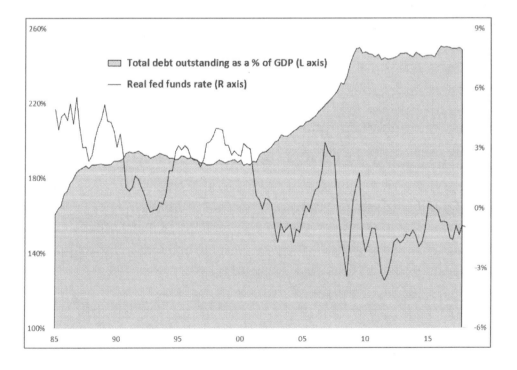

I firmly believe that, since 2002, the Federal Reserve's primary policy concern has been the large debt burden carried by the US. This fear caused the Fed to set its funds rate artificially low to make that debt burden more affordable. For example, I estimate that without the Fed's extraordinary behavior, US homeowners would be paying an extra $200 billion a year in mortgage interest, or over 2% of their income. Big difference.

Opposing the debt finance worry is the positive lending environment of low loan losses. That's an environment in which the Federal Reserve normally raises the fed funds rate, and when the time value of money is *above* normal.

How will the tug of war evolve over the next three years? Towards investors, I expect. Between now and 2021, I expect the 1-year time value to rise from 0% at present to 0.5% to 1.0%, and the ten-year time value to rise from 0.5% to 1.5%, for three reasons:

The Federal Reserve governors currently believe that the normal nominal rate (they call it the "central tendency") for fed funds is 3%, the same as my estimate. The 1.7% mid-2018 rate is therefore substantially below normal even in the eyes of the Fed, and they seem serious about reaching their target by the end of 2019 in response to a healthy economy, low unemployment and recent fiscal stimulus (a.k.a. tax cuts and government spending increases).

Further, I expect total US debt growth to rise faster than its speed limit for the next few years. And I expect inflation to trend up, as I'll explain next. As a result, the 1-year CD is a not a great investment now, but should improve over the next three years.

My Inflation Forecast: Rising

IN CHAPTER FOUR, I IDENTIFIED four key economic drivers of inflation. Let's review how these drivers are likely to behave in the next three years.

First is banks' willingness to lend, which is part of the debt cycle. We know that banks are perfectly willing to lend today, and, as I said above, I expect them to continue to feel this way for at least another year or two. So that's a plus for higher inflation.

Second, wage rates should rise. The unemployment rate is currently very low (below 4%), giving employees increasing bargaining power. Then there is the current political pressure to limit competition to US workers—the "America First" slogan is aimed at employees, not businesses. America First tactics are to shrink imports, expel undocumented workers, and reduce legal immigration. Fewer workers available for employers to choose from means more money in workers' pockets. For example, in October, 2017, department store Target raised its minimum wage to $11 an hour, and promised $15 an hour by 2020. Walmart followed with its own minimum $11 per hour pay. And teachers in several states have been on strike recently for higher pay.

Figure 9.2 shows that the low unemployment rate has pushed real wage growth (after inflation) to 1%, at the higher end of the range for the Great Modernization era. I expect an even lower unemployment rate to drive 2% real wage growth rate at some point over the next three years.

Figure 9.2. Real wage growth is already near its Great Modernization era high. I expect it to hit 2% at some point during the next three years. (Sources: Wages— BEA. Inflation and unemployment rates—BLS.)

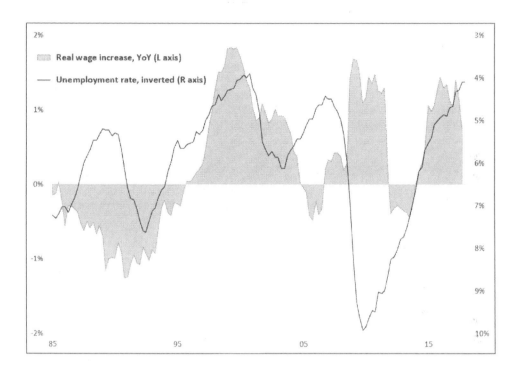

Third, import volume growth has slowed, and is likely to slow further. Figure 9.3 shows a history of real (after-inflation) imports.

Figure 9.3. The pace of real annual import growth slowed from 5-10% during 1990-2005 to 3-4% today. (Sources: Imports—BEA. Inflation—BLS.)

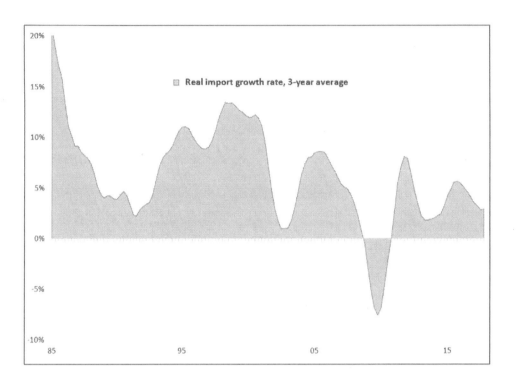

As I said in chapter four, imports restrain inflation. The pace of import growth has already slowed to the 3% to 4% range, a decline from 5% to 10% during 1990-2005. The current administration is determined to see that number decline further, through tariffs, trade pact renegotiations, publicly calling out companies that outsource, and lowering the US corporate tax rate.

Put down another plus for higher inflation.

Fourth, oil prices are determined by a complex set of supply-and-demand variables that I am far from expert on. But in my humble view, the price per barrel of oil for the next few years shouldn't stray too far from its recent $60 to $70 price range. The huge boom in US shale drilling has created global excess capacity. Voluntary production cuts by OPEC were needed to drain the excess supply of oil. The voluntary oil production cuts will fade if oil prices rise further. And energy from natural gas, solar, and wind are all growing. On the flip side, energy demand is growing rapidly in China and India. On balance, I'll leave oil prices as neutral for inflation.

My inflation forecast. Putting together the above four factors, I expect the inflation rate to rise from about 2% in mid-2018 to 2.5% to 3% within the next three years. I also expect the longer-term inflation outlook, which today is 2.3%, to rise a bit too, to about 2.5%. Technology (driverless cars, robots, big data) has the power to turn the price curve downward at some point, but probably not soon enough to influence your current investment decisions.

My Earnings Growth Forecast: Slowing

I HAVE SHOWN THAT PRIVATE SECTOR DEBT growth is the major driver of GDP and business earnings growth. So if we want to predict the direction of corporate earnings, we need to forecast private sector debt growth. Let's do it.

As a reminder, Figure 9.4 (on the next page) shows the private sector debt cycle.

I again begin the private sector debt story with the loan loss boxes. Is today's US economy closer to the upper left or the lower right of the debt cycle?

Figure 9.4. The private sector debt cycle.

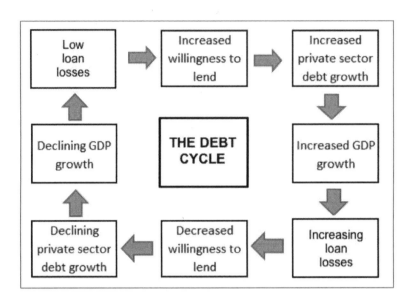

I of course seek answers from real data. The data for early 2018 shows that the banking industry's total charge-off ratio (loan losses as a percent of all loans outstanding) is near historic lows (Figure 9.5).

Figure 9.5. Bank loan charge-off rates are currently near historic lows, although the bottom of the cycle has likely passed. (Source: Fed.)

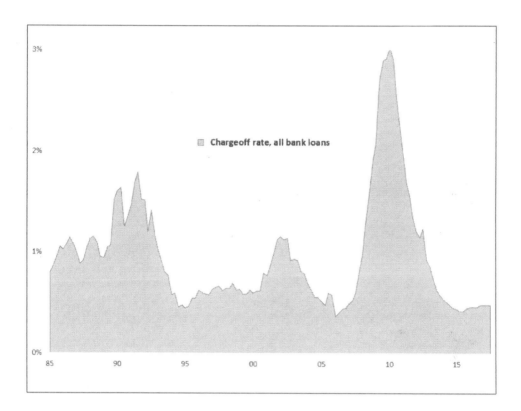

This fact starts us in the upper left-hand corner of the debt cycle graphic. As usual at this point in the cycle, private sector lenders should feel comfortable lending because of low loss rates. Private sector debt growth should therefore be booming, right? But Figure 9.6 tells a different story.

Figure 9.6. Real private sector debt growth has been modest in the current debt cycle, and it even slowed over the past year. (Sources: Debt data—Fed. Inflation—BLS.)

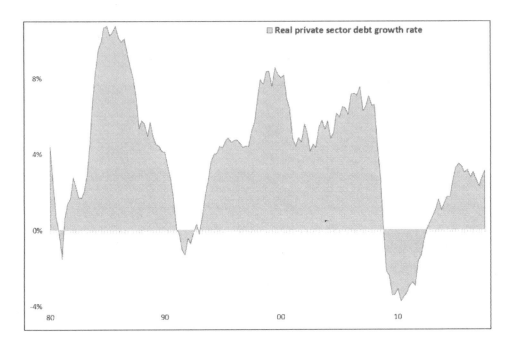

Real private sector debt growth been historically slow since the end of the Great Recession, and the pace of growth actually declined over the past year. Why haven't low loss rates translated into stronger debt growth? Unfortunately for us students of history, it never precisely repeats itself. The recent private debt growth story has two new wrinkles unseen in prior cycles.

One wrinkle is that lenders today have fewer new customers available to them than they used to. Figure 9.7 shows that both consumer and business debt levels, while off from their peaks, are currently well above historic norms. More debt already on the books means less debt that can safely be added to those books.

Figure 9.7. Part of the reason for this cycle's weak private sector debt growth is that debt levels as a percent of GDP are already historically high. (Sources: GDP— BEA. Debt data—Fed.)

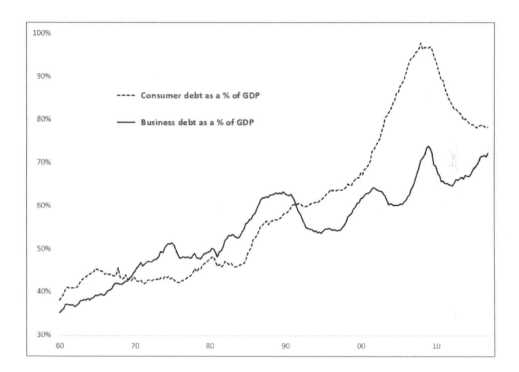

Second, bank and other lending regulations were tightened a lot in response to the 2008-2009 financial crisis. A good way to summarize the impact of lending regulation is to look at the financial system's leverage. Banks are required by regulations to back their loans and other assets with defined minimum amounts of shareholders' equity, or capital. Financial leverage is calculated as the ratio of the loan and other assets a bank holds to the amount of capital it has.

Let's use JP Morgan as an example. The assets-to-capital ratio at this US megabank was roughly 12 during the boom years from 2000 to 2007. For example, at the end of 2007, JP Morgan held $1.6 trillion in assets (that's a lot, right?) and $123 billion in shareholders' equity. But after the debt bubble burst, the government passed the Dodd-Frank law, which limited bank leverage in order to reduce the risk of another taxpayer bailout of the banking system. Since 2008, JP Morgan's leverage ratio has averaged about eight, and despite current low loss rates, it dipped to 7.5 by March, 2018. Note that this decline in bank leverage parallels the decline in money velocity I discussed back in chapter seven.

In sum, while private sector debt loss rates are low, banks and other lenders have been restrained from growing debt as much as they normally do at this point in the debt cycle.

Forecasting the Private Sector Debt Cycle Three Years Out: Slowing

WHAT WILL 2021 BRING? Perhaps a new president. Maybe another Kardashian sex change. Maybe daffodil will be the "it" color.

Sadly, none of these issues is the topic of this book. My more pedestrian question is "How fast will private-sector debt be growing in 2021?" My view is that by then, the US will have moved through the "increasing private sector debt growth" box, to reach the "rising loan losses" box. As a result, private sector debt growth in 2021 should be slowing. Forecasting by lending products, I see two negatives and one positive.

The first negative I see is auto and credit card lending. Their loss rates have already started to rise thanks to several years of above-the-speed-limit loan growth. History says that above-the-speed-limit growth persists until loss rates are much higher than they are today. For example, credit card issuer Synchrony in its second quarter earnings conference call on July 21, 2017, said that, despite a rise in its loss rate, it aimed to ramp up its loan growth to 10%. Nutty, but remember those animal spirits. So, by 2021, both credit card and auto loan losses should be notably higher, and loan growth should have slowed materially.

The other likely negative is business lending. Business debt has been growing above its speed limit for the past four years. Bond investors are getting both complacent and desperate—complacent about economic growth and desperate for yield. For example, consider this quote from *The Wall Street Journal* (December 27, 2017):

> Investors are clamoring for leveraged loans as years of low interest rates and central banks' bond buying have pushed down returns elsewhere. Trillions of dollars of sovereign debt, primarily in Europe, continue to sport negative yields, meaning investors pay to lend governments money. With "far too much cash trying to find too few homes," private-equity firms "can be more aggressive and lenders will take it," said Adam Freeman, a partner at Linklaters LLP.

Low current losses should allow the business lenders' fast driving to keep going for a little while more. But, by 2021, defaults should be picking up nicely, and business lenders should be tightening their lending standards.

The positive I see for debt growth is home mortgages. Their growth should ramp up from the paltry current 3% rate to about 5% by 2021. Logically, lenders today should be falling over themselves to make home mortgage loans, for two reasons. First, existing homeowners have a record $14 trillion of equity in their homes to serve as collateral for new debt. Second, housing is in somewhat short supply nationally. All that is needed is for the current political administration to loosen bank regulations, which it seems happy to do.

To wrap up, I expect private sector debt growth should accelerate over the next year or two, but three years from now rising loan defaults should be reversing that direction. In 2021, I expect overall real private sector debt growth to be onlyabout 1.5%.

The New Earnings Growth Variable: Government Debt

IN CHAPTER SIX, I IGNORED GOVERNMENT DEBT as a key driver of economic and investment cycles, explaining that government debt is generally counter-cyclical to private sector debt (Figure 6.12). But as it turns out, this time is different. For the foreseeable future, government debt growth should be "pro-cyclical"; that is, it will rise despite solid private sector debt growth. As a result, economic and business earnings growth should be better than indicated just by my normal tracking of private sector debt. Figure 9.8 shows that the Congressional Budget Office's (CBO) forecast of federal government deficits as a percent of GDP is expected to be higher than normal despite assumed healthy GDP growth.

Figure 9.8. The forecast federal government deficit as a share of GDP is quite high, and is by far a record for an expected non-recessionary period. Why? (Source: Congressional Budget Office.)

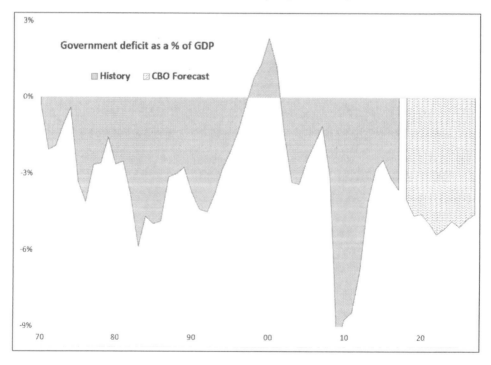

As both a citizen and an investor, you should be asking, "Why the booming deficit?" Here's why:

First, the Baby Boomers keep sticking it to us. They are so smug, those Baby Boomers, with their Woodstock memories and tie-dye shirts and Motown. Now they are retiring, in droves, to their hippie communes in Boca Raton— apparently at the pace of about 10,000 a day. The government makes financial promises to retirees, in the form of Social Security and Medicare. Payroll taxes are supposed to cover those costs, but those infernal Baby Boomers are overwhelming the system. (Okay, politicians are to blame for overpromising, but that's another story). The CBO estimates that future costs of Social Security, Medicare, and federal government retiree programs, less payroll taxes, will rise from about $400 billion a year now to *over $1 trillion* by 2025.

Second, interest costs are set to explode. Stimulative Federal Reserve policy has resulted in the federal government paying only about 2% on its debt at present. As a result, today's $17 trillion of government debt costs taxpayers only slightly more than the $4 trillion of debt in 2000. But by 2027, federal debt outstanding will be at least $27 trillion, according to the CBO. And if I am right, the cost of that debt should be much higher.

The 5-year Treasury bond yield, which has proven to be a reasonable proxy for the average cost of federal government debt, is about 2.5% today. Since the 5-year Treasury historically yields about one percentage point more than fed funds, if fed funds rise to about 3.5%, which I expect, the 5-year yield should reach 4.5%. In that case, federal government interest payments would rise to nearly *$1 trillion a year* by 2027, up from about $300 billion this year. That's two $1 trillions. They're starting to add up.

Third, taxes were just cut and spending just increased. Rational policy-makers, knowing that the current annual government deficit is already about $500 billion and that retirement and interest costs will soar over the next decade, would be tightening the nation's belt, and even looking for ways to reduce government spending. But as I keep reminding you, we just aren't very rational. Instead, in late 2017, annual tax payments were cut by

$150 billion a year, and military and other spending was raised by a similar amount. Rack up another $300 billion a year to the deficit. What the heck?

The result of these three facts is that the federal deficit will add more than normal to economic growth and business profits. And of course more to debt than normal. Good for stocks, bad for bonds.

My Market Risk Forecast: Investors Are Pretty Optimistic at Present

RECALL FROM CHAPTER TWO THAT MY STOCK VALUATION is based on this formula:

$$\frac{\text{Earnings per share}}{\text{Stock price}} = \text{10-year Treasury bond yield} + \text{market risk} - \text{earnings growth}$$

That's five variables. At any given time, actual numbers for three of the variables are available: the S&P 500 index price, current S&P 500 earnings per share, and the 10-year Treasury bond yield. I then fill in my forecasted earnings growth driver, namely 2020 private sector debt growth.

That leaves just market risk as an unknown. Let's solve for it, shall we? The magic of algebra gives us:

$$\text{Market risk} = \frac{\text{Earnings per share}}{\text{Stock price}} - \text{10-year Treasury bond yield} + \text{debt growth}$$

The resulting historical market risk values are shown in Figure 9.9.

Figure 9.9. A history of my estimate of market risk. (Sources: S&P 500 price – Yahoo Finance. S&P 500 earnings – S&P. 10-year Treasury yield – Fed. GDP deflator – BEA. Private sector debt growth – Fed.)

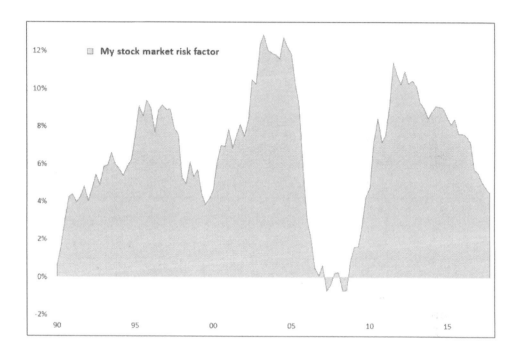

The variations in market risk shown in Figure 9.9 measure the amount of confidence or fear that investors have about the future. The value of this market risk measure is well summarized in a saying popularized by investing god Warren Buffett: "Be fearful when others are greedy and greedy when others are fearful." Stocks are usually a good buy when investors are scared and a good sell when they are very confident.

In fact, Figure 9.10 shows that is exactly what has happened historically. From each market risk data point, I measured the annual change in the S&P 500 stock index over the following three years. I found a very good correlation: the higher the currently perceived market risk, the greater the future returns.

Figure 9.10. The greater the perceived market risk, the greater the stock market performance over the next three years. (Sources: S&P 500 price – Yahoo Finance. S&P 500 earnings – S&P. 10-year Treasury yield – Fed. GDP deflator – BEA. Private sector debt growth – Fed.)

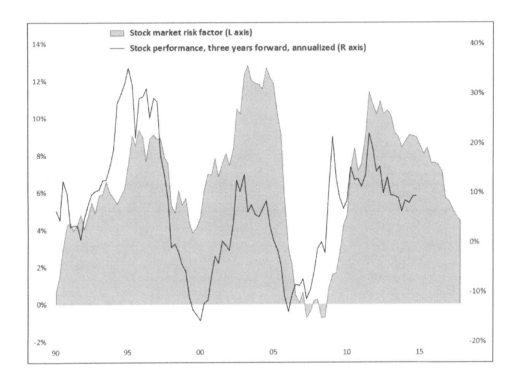

If my private sector debt growth forecast is close to right, then current perceived market risk is somewhat optimistic, and therefore stock market returns over the next few years should be below average.

What Debt Cycle Investing Suggests for Today's Asset Allocation

NOW IT'S TIME TO PUT THE INVESTMENT VARIABLE FORECASTS I've just reviewed to work by addressing whether you should underweight or overweight cash, bonds, and stocks as of today—meaning mid-2018.

Let's start with a benchmark. In the introduction to this book, I mentioned the standard 60/40 rule. That rule recommends an asset allocation of 60% in stocks and 40% in bonds for the "average" investor. To make room for cash investments, I'll change the standard to 55% stocks, 35% bonds, and 10% cash. That's a general starting point, although it may not be yours because of your different age, financial situation, and other circumstances, as I discussed in chapter one. With that said, here goes.

The Cash Investment Outlook

I FORECAST ABOUT a 0.5% to 1.0% short-term time value and a 2.5% to 3% inflation rate by 2021. That adds up to a 3.5% CD rate three years from now, or a roughly 2.5% annual return over the three years.

The Bond Outlook

THE YIELD ON THE 10-YEAR TREASURY BOND at mid-2018 was 3.0%, consisting of a 2.3% expected long-term inflation rate and a 0.7% long-term time value of money. I earlier forecast above a 2.5% to 3.0% expected inflation rate and a 1.5% long-term time value of money. That sums to a 4.0-% to 4.5% forecast yield on the 10-year Treasury bond in 2021.

If I am right, the value of a 3.0% 10-year Treasury purchased today would have to fall by about 10% by 2021. Three years of interest at 3.0% less a 10% decline in value leaves a three-year total return of about 0%. Not good.

The Stock Outlook

TO FORECAST STOCK RETURNS THROUGH 2021, I refer back to figure 9.10. It says that perceived market risk is on the low side today, so stock returns should be modest over the next three years. My earnings yield valuation tool calculates that the average annual stock return should be about 4%. Please note that my valuation tool, like others', is not a micrometer. While I believe that a 4% expected annual stock return is a useful central tendancy, the actual result could be notably higher or lower. Significant deviations could occur for a variety of reasons—surprising Federal Reserve policy, surprising debt growth, a political regime change, war, pestilence, the arrival of the Messiah, and so on.

Relative Value and a Recommended Asset Allocation

SUMMARIZING, CASH HAS AN EXPECTED ANNUAL RETURN over the next three years of 2.5%, bonds of 0%, and stocks of 4%. Stocks should therefore be overweighted and bonds underweighted. But by how much?

Adjusting my three-bucket standard allocation by just a few percentage points is pointless; if you like stocks now, moving from 55%/35%/10% to 57%/33%/10% isn't going to change your investment returns materially. I therefore recommend a mix today for the average investor of 70% stocks, 5% bonds, 25% cash.

I could see reducing bonds all the way to zero because their risk/reward is so unattractive, but I'll assume that you, your stockbroker, or a waiter at your favorite diner has identified a few muni or corporate bonds that make sense to you. To cut your risk of overweighting stocks (remember, they have the most volatile returns), I add to cash.

The Sad Truth: A Near-Term Future
of Limited Absolute Investment Returns

MY ASSET ALLOCATION ANALYSIS SUGGESTS that even an optimal mix of investments still will return only 3% a year over the next three years. Why so low?

To answer that question, I'm going to recall my first witness, Figure I.2, now renamed Figure 9.11, and add a data series.

Figure 9.11. I noted two current investment extremes in chapter one: Federal Reserve policy and debt levels. Here I add a third: corporate profit margins. (Sources: Debt and fed funds—Fed. GDP, business profits and national income— BEA.)

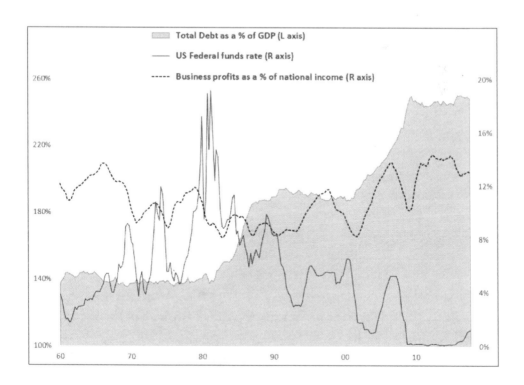

The fact is that US investors today have to grapple with no fewer than three investment extremes:

- Debt outstanding: It is dangerous to materially increase the US's current 250% ratio of total debt to GDP.
- Fed funds: There is scant room to lower the Federal Reserve's current 1.7% fed funds rate, and loads of upside. And the Fed already owns $4 trillion of government debt.
- Business profit margins: They are near record levels at present. Could they be vulnerable to a strengthening power of labor? Or to the impact of trade wars?

Current investment valuations reflect these extremes already, with the 1-year CD rate at a low 0.4%, the 10-year Treasury bond yield at a low 3.0%, and an above-average stock market P/E ratio of 16. Regression to the mean says that all of these positive extremes will have to moderate at some point. It therefore seems likely that investment returns over the next decade will be materially lower than those we have become used to. I am not alone in this pessimism on future investment returns. For example, the previously cited investment guru Jeremy Grantham said in last year's third quarter investment letter:

> . . . A traditional, diversified 65% stock/35% fixed income portfolio today . . . I believe is likely to produce a return over 10 years in the 1% to 3% real range.

A quick look at Japan's experience is instructive. While Japan is not the US—for example, it currently has no population growth, it supports a far smaller military and it consumes far more fish per capita—both are modern industrial countries with lots of debt. Figure 9.12 shows a history of Japan's ratio of private sector debt to GDP, as well as the Nikkei 225 stock price index, which is their equivalent of the S&P 500 index.

Figure 9.12. Japan's long-term deleveraging from a severe private sector debt bubble weighed heavily on its stock market for a long time. (Sources: Debt—International Bank for Settlements. Nikkei 225—Nikkei Industry Research Institute.)

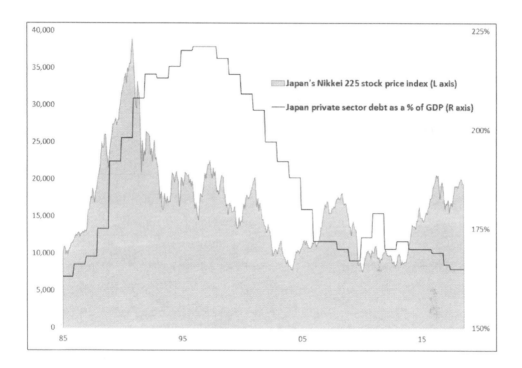

The picture shows that Japan's private sector debt ratio peaked in around 1995. By then, its version of the fed funds rate was already under 1%. Twenty-three years later, Japan's stock prices are the same as they were in 1995. To keep the economy chugging along since then, Japan's government debt has grown by leaps and bounds, and its central bank has been the most aggressive in the world in keeping interest rates low and buying bonds and even stocks.

The lesson I get by applying Japan's experience to the US today is that our investment return expectations should be low, and probably far lower than you hope for and plan for. For example, a poll of the crowd at an investment conference I recently attended said the audience expected an average annual investment return of 6% to 7% over the next decade.

What Could Change?

OF COURSE, AS I'VE EMPHASIZED throughout this book, economic conditions are in constant flux, which means your asset allocation decisions also need to be continually reconsidered. By the time you read these pages, some of the forecast I just presented is likely already outdated. Actual results could be either better or worse than my central forecast.

What could change? Let's start with the optimistic scenarios.

Views on risk could get even more complacent. One thing I have definitely learned over time: Investors rarely stop at stupid, they usually go to insane. Some quick anecdotes:

In 1986, my first year as a stock analyst, I learned that office vacancy rates were at 15%, up from 3% in 1980. "That seems like a pretty dangerous sign for commercial real estate," I said to myself. The blow-up didn't occur until after three more years of over-building and over-lending.

On December 12, 1996, Federal Reserve Chairman Alan "Five Fingers" Greenspan famously wondered whether "irrational exuberance has unduly escalated asset values." Over the next three years, the tech-heavy NASDAQ stock index more than doubled, before falling back to its original level three years later.

By the spring of 2005, housing affordability reached a historical low and home sales peaked. Over the next two years, lenders took on another $2 trillion of home mortgage debt, a good deal of it subprime.

GoPro makes cameras—you know, those things that are on just about every cell phone in the US? That didn't stop the market from going nuts when GoPro went public in 2014. The stock opened at $24 a share. Within three months, it reached $94. It is now about $6 and is expected to lose money in 2018.

Based on a lifetime of observing irrational behavior like this, when I ask myself, "Could lenders continue to grow faster than speed limits even though their losses are rising?" my answer is "Sure." And could what looks like an expensive stock market rise another 20% over the next year or two? Again, sure.

Business profit margins could go also higher, for several reasons. One positive I expect to continue is management discipline. The drive for increased efficiency is pretty much encoded in the DNA of business leaders these days. One example is Boeing. Even though this aircraft manufacturer has only one real competitor (Airbus), the company recently underwent a series of cost reductions that boosted earnings and sent the stock soaring. And private equity and activist investor funds currently have record levels of cash to invest, so stupid managements don't have the luxury of staying around for long.

Another continued positive for corporate profits should be industry consolidation. Almost every week brings news of the merger of two major companies in some industry. More consolidation = less competition = more profits . . . a capitalist's dream.

Third, large corporate tax cuts were signed into law in December, 2017. Businesses are likely to hang on to a good deal of the extra earnings for the benefit of shareholders.

Finally, automation seems on the verge of another leap forward. Robots, self-driving vehicles and big data. They all replace employees with cheaper machines, to business' benefit.

Now for the dark side.

Business profits could go lower. Yes, I know I just said the opposite, but labor costs could be a problem. Unemployment is currently quite low. And clearly a lot of Americans are upset with their financial circumstances. A material increase in wage inflation seems logical, to businesses' detriment. Another profit risk is what I'll call the "Amazon syndrome": sales growth at the expense of profits. A certain class of investors loves this strategy. For example, rapidly growing online furniture retailer Wayfair is expected (at least by Morgan Stanley) to lose money until 2025. Or consider that icon Uber managed to lose $4.5 billion in 2017. Could selling more to lose more spread to more companies? Possible.

Trade wars could break out. While here in the States we talk about America First, our foreign rivals believe in England First, China First, and very likely Ivory Coast First. A breakdown of international trade agreements due to a surge in nationalism could materially slow global GDP growth.

Actual wars could break out. There are a lot of angry people out there, from North Korea to Iran to Ukraine to some in the US. Angry words can obviously lead to angry actions. Investors aren't crazy about wars.

In short, human societies are volatile and difficult to predict. Even the most astute forecast is unlikely to remain viable for long. How can you use my method to adjust your asset allocation as circumstances evolve? That's the topic of my final chapter.

10 How to Be a Debt Cycle Investor in the Years to Come

THE PREVIOUS CHAPTER CONCLUDED BY RECOMMENDING an asset allocation as of mid-2018 of 70% stocks, 5% bonds, and 25% cash. But time doesn't stand still. Summer becomes fall, Monday becomes Thursday (if Monday was the beginning of a three-day bender) and the big debt-cycle wheel keep on turnin'. So how should you manage asset allocation shifts going forward?

In one of two ways. The easiest, I modestly propose, is to visit my web site garygordoninvesting.com, where I will continuously update you on relevant news stories and other asset allocation issues. I'll work hard to keep your weekly reading to ten minutes or less.

Another way is to do the research yourself. It can be done. To do so, follow the Four Whats. No, not the Motown group from the 1960s. (Okay, the Four Tops, you got me.) The Four Whats outline my approach to gathering information needed for considering asset allocation shifts. They are *what to ask, what to read, what to believe,* and *what to do with the facts.*

What to Ask

YOUR RESEARCH SHOULD FOCUS ON GETTING UPDATES on the following issues, which I identified in chapters four and five as driving the key investment variables.

- Most important, where is the US in its debt cycle? I've argued in this book that, as of mid-2018, America is still in the low-loan-loss, debt-growth phase. Is there new evidence that corroborates my view or disputes it?

- Is Federal Reserve policy changing? Is the time value of your money improving or worsening?
- How is inflation changing? In particular, what is happening with the factors that most significantly impact inflation—the debt cycle, wages, imports, and oil prices?
- Is the level of business risk changing? Are US companies continuing to leverage up? Are there signs that the leveraging has reached a point where loan losses should start rising?
- Are business profit margins changing? Are US companies, in aggregate, maintaining their profit discipline, or are they competing too hard for growth or other goals and thereby losing their focus on maintaining profit levels?

What to Read

IF I HAD TO PICK A SINGLE SOURCE OF INFORMATION, I'd say *The Wall Street Journal*. This is an unpaid plug that says nothing about my politics. The fact is that, as a business newspaper, the *Journal* regularly addresses all of the issues I want data on.

But you may be familiar with this new-fangled thing called the Internet. In the modern world, you don't have to rely on a single source or even just a few sources to efficiently gather data. Type topics like "debt growth" or "Federal Reserve policy" into your browser, and many useful sources will pop up. Also some strange porn sites, but stay focused people.

What to Believe

NOW IT GETS INTERESTING. What you're looking for are facts, not opinion or spin. The media are in the business of getting our attention, so they frequently try to be controversial, play on our biases, or appeal to our emotions.

And we bring our own emotional biases even to stories that are strictly factual. So in your research, try as much as possible to zero in on actual numbers from reliable sources. And then, crucially, accept these facts even when they conflict with your beliefs. That is why I created all of the pictures in this book: Focusing on the data limits the emotional noise. Finding new data has often caused me to change my views. And the more data I see on the same topic, the greater the chance that I can trust the data and identify a real pattern or trend.

For these reasons, I skip opinion pieces. I also skip forecasts, even forecasts by seemingly reliable sources. Give me the facts, ma'am, just the facts. I'll do my own forecasting.

What to Do with the Facts: Research by Anecdote

LIKE ALL LIFE, ECONOMIC ACTIVITY IS AMAZINGLY COMPLICATED. Rarely do we get a simple "A, therefore B." Rather, we get "A, B, D, E, and F, but not C, which probably points to Z." Unlike arithmetic, life doesn't usually provide us with a clear cause-and-effect formula. Instead, it gives us stories that suggest connections that vary in clarity and strength.

Recognizing these realities, I call my data-collection approach *research by anecdote*. When you see a number of facts pointing in the same direction, you may be on to a trend. If the facts seem to conflict, withhold judgment and wait for more data to turn up. You don't have to get enough facts to create charts like the ones I've used in this book. The charts are great teachers; we can now use anecdotes to apply what we've learned from the charts.

A story from my working days as a stock analyst may be helpful in illustrating how research by anecdote works. In the early 1990s, I was covering the mortgage lending industry. From 1990 to 1993, the mortgage rate declined from 10% to 7%, setting off one of the first refinancing waves. Mortgage originations surged from $562 billion in 1991 to $1 trillion in 1993, an 82% increase. A number of privately-held mortgage bankers took advantage of their booming profits to go public, and I picked up stock research coverage on several of them.

But economic activity is cyclical. In early 1994, the Federal Reserve began raising the fed funds rate. Mortgage rates began rising as well, and it was easy to forecast that the mortgage refinancing boom was going to die. In fact, in 1995, loan origination volume 37% below its 1993 level.

As a stock analyst, I needed to get a feel for how the industry was going to handle the slowdown. There was no single source to which I could turn for the answer, so I sought anecdotes. I asked managers at the mortgage companies I knew what their plans were when industry volume slowed. They all gave a version of the same answer: "We only represent 1% of mortgage lending now, so we'll go to 2%."

Well, when 100 lenders with a 1% share all want to grow to 2%, that sums to 200% of market share. Sorry, but that's not happening. It was easy to conclude that the lenders were going to do stupid things in their attempt to achieve the impossible. In the lending world, "stupid" means underpricing the product or making too-risky loans. They did both, and most went out of business. The research by anecdote ended up predicting the future quite accurately.

As a side note, this period offers a wonderful example of irrational behavior by supposedly rational beings. The big banks should have seen the industry downturn as a great chance to watch their smaller competitors with far less financial resources fail, then to grab market share after the failures. But inexplicitly, the banks started *buying* these companies, often for big money. Without naming names, when Big Bank A bought Independent Banker B in early 1994 for $300 million, it bragged that it would *triple* the earnings of Independent Banker B within a year.

A year later, I ran into the former president of Independent Banker B. "How's it going?" I asked. "Oh, they shut us down and we were all laid off." $300 million down the drain. In a year!

Research by Anecdote—Some Recent Examples

I'LL NOW BRING MY EXPLANATION of the research-by-anecdote process up to date. I've collected several media stories and data sources printed in early August, 2017. I'll use them to show you how I go through my process of culling the wheat (actual new facts) from the chaff (opinion, or examples of irrational thinking and behavior) in order to get answers to the key questions I listed earlier in this chapter.

Example 1: Home Mortgage Lending

ON AUGUST 4, 2017, *The Los Angeles Times* printed this headline: "As Prices Rise, Mortgage Lenders Are Making it Easier to Buy a House."

Home mortgage lending standards are a very important component of the debt cycle. Over $9 trillion of home mortgage debt is outstanding in the US, and, as I discussed earlier, originating more of it boosts the economy in two ways—by generating more home construction and by enabling more consumer spending financed by home equity loans.

You've learned in this book that lending is driven far more by changing loan underwriting standards than by changing interest rates. Investors therefore need to learn into whether mortgage lending standards are easing or tightening.

The headline above suggests easing. What facts does the article present to support this claim? I scanned the 60-paragraph story (did they fire *all* of the editors at the *LA Times*?) to find useful nuggets. The first one I noticed was this:

> . . . Changes in the mortgage industry are afoot, with the goal of loosening some of the strict standards established after the subprime crisis . . . Said William E. Brown, the president of the National Assn. of Realtors, the industry is "trying to give them more options to buy a house."

So someone knowledgeable about the lending process—the head of the realtors' trade association—says that lenders are easing up. Interesting. But did the article offer any factual examples of actual loan underwriting changes being made? Yes, it did. Here's one:

> After the housing crisis, Fannie Mae established a debt-to-income cap of 45%, except for those who put at least 20% down . . . Last month, Fannie did away with those special requirements, raising its cap to 50% . . .

The article also noted other mortgage-rule easing by Fannie Mae and Freddie Mac, including lower down payments. Are changes like these enough to move the needle of mortgage debt growth? Yes, they are, according to a credible source:

> A recent analysis by the Urban Institute called Fannie's new policy "a win for expanding access to credit" and estimated it would lead to 95,000 new loans being approved annually nationwide.

This data is very helpful because it gives a little sense of the size of the potential lending increase from the underwriting changes. With an average mortgage size in the US somewhat over $200,000, this underwriting change can generate over $20 billion of new debt. In fact, this article from a year ago turned out to be dead-on. Since then, the percentage of Fannie Mae loans made with more than a 45% debt-to-income ratio rose from 5% to 20%.

The article gave another reason for easing lending standards—competition:

> Also, lenders are moving to relax some standards partly because they fear losing business as home prices and mortgage rates rise, said Guy Cecala, publisher of Inside Mortgage Finance. "If your business is going to drop 20%," he said, "you need to come up with ways to offset that."

The greater the competition in any business, the greater the likelihood that one or more players will do something stupid in order to survive. So this quote raises a warning flag. How worried should we be that home-mortgage lending standards are already loose enough to imminently generate higher loan losses? Another nugget in the story says, "Not too worried":

> For all the changes, Laurie Goodman of the Urban Institute characterized them as "very marginal." According to an Urban Institute index loans today are less risky than from 2000 to 2002, a time period when Goodman considered lending standards reasonable.

I happen to have worked with Laurie and I trust her completely, but even if you've never heard of her before, the fact that she works at a reputable place and seems to have done her homework should give you confidence. Finally, the article presents one emotional fantasy, as the following quotation shows:

> The changes . . . have brought criticism from some corners that liberalizing rules for down payments and how much debt a borrower can have is a slippery slope that could eventually lead to another bubble. "This is what happened last time," said Edward Pinto, a fellow at the American Enterprise Institute, a conservative think tank.

A "conservative" or a "liberal" think tank is very likely to view every issue through the emotional lens of politics. I therefore categorize the above quotation as a useless opinion rather than a useful fact—and I ignore it.

Net/net, this article presented compelling evidence that the rate of home mortgage debt growth should be increasing. Good for stocks, bad for bonds.

Example 2: Debt Outstanding

AH, THE FEDERAL RESERVE FINANCIAL ACCOUNTS of the United States—the Great American Novel of the economy! Also known as Z.1, or the Flow of Funds report, it has it all—a long list of characters whose fortunes ebb and flow over time; comedy, tragedy, horror, love stories (mostly about the love of money)—all presented in the form of 184 dense tables. Who can resist such compelling reading?

Actually, most people find it very easy to resist. Even I, uber-nerd that I am, have not plumbed the depths of all 184 tables. No man, woman, or child could plumb them without risking the loony bin. But a few pages tell a good deal of the story. That's why I recommend you overcome your instincts and take a peek at the Federal Reserve website.

Click on the "Data" tab on top and then the "Financial Accounts of the United States—Z.1" tab below. Start with pages 6, 7, 138, and 141. Pages 6 and 7 present debt data, while 138 and 141 display household balance sheets and how they change. And perhaps end there, too, if you've already broken out in a cold sweat.

Figure 10.1 shows a section of the most recent update to a table that is vital to our analysis of the debt cycle—debt growth by economic sector. It is found on page i of the Financial Accounts.

Figure 10.1. A portion of the debt growth summary table in the Federal Reserve's Financial Accounts of the United States report.

	Total LA384104005	Total LA154104005	Households Home mortgage LA153165105	Consumer credit LA153166000	Business Total LA144104005	Corporate LA104104005	Federal government LA314104005
2010	37284.0	13574.8	9985.3	2646.8	9994.7	6043.9	10528.6
2011	38449.8	13381.0	9769.5	2757.8	10257.2	6370.6	11667.3
2012	40194.3	13443.7	9558.4	2919.7	10760.4	6702.9	12847.8
2013	41632.8	13596.0	9474.6	3095.6	11244.4	7082.3	13705.1
2014	43383.9	13953.1	9455.8	3317.4	11941.2	7497.9	14441.1
2015	45185.9	14216.9	9586.1	3417.2	12745.6	7996.2	15165.6
2016	47218.1	14671.3	9794.4	3645.2	13449.8	8393.0	16008.3
2017	49050.7	15251.4	10085.1	3841.1	14259.3	8947.8	16455.3

Here's some of what we can learn from Figure 10.1.

Growth of total debt outstanding in the US appears in the first column. The Fed officially calls it "total domestic nonfinancial debt." This is the debt definition that correlates to GDP, and that should be the driver of your asset allocation decision. The nominal (pre-inflation) 2017 growth rate was 3.8%. The table shows that's pretty modest. It supports my view that while loan losses are currently low, debt growth hasn't entered its speculative growth phase yet.

Household credit includes home mortgages, credit cards, student loans, and auto loans. Aficionados can find details of these forms of debt on pages 127 and 129 of Z.1. Household debt is showing some signs of acceleration, mostly because home mortgage debt growth is returning to normal.

So far, so good. But remember one of my key principles of data analysis: *All data must be questioned.*

Take a look at the federal government column. It suggests that federal government debt growth materially decelerated last year to 2.8%. That doesn't jibe with media reports of still-high federal deficits.

My uber-nerd sleuthing found the answer on page 83, which gives a snapshot of the federal government balance sheet. It shows that the federal government shifted about $200 billion of debt from its own account to its federal pension fund account (don't ask me how or why). A truer federal government debt growth estimate for 2017 was 4%.

I conclude from my page 7 review that the US has room for accelerating debt growth in this cycle, which is good for stocks and bad for bonds.

Example 3: Construction Employment

HERE'S A HEADLINE FROM THE AUGUST 8, 2017, *Wall Street Journal*: "Construction-Worker Shortage Worsens in June."

At a glance, this article appears relevant to our inflation questions. A labor shortage normally requires the industry to increase wages to get the workers it needs. And higher construction wages should mean higher home prices. The article presents these supporting facts:

> The number of open construction jobs increased to a seasonally adjusted 225,000 in June from 163,000 in May, according to the Labor Department. That is the most open jobs since September 2016 and significantly more than the 171,000 open jobs reported a year ago, according to Robert Dietz, chief economist at the National Association of Home Builders.

This is important news, right? Maybe not. The article continues as follows:

> The number of open construction jobs, a measure that can be volatile from month to month, has increased throughout the economic expansion but more recently has shown signs of leveling off.

If the numbers are volatile, and recent data shows a "leveling off" of open construction jobs, then I can't be certain that I have a fact here. This is a good example of why you can't simply rely on a headline, or even on data that is presented. Media stories are meant to be catchy—accuracy not required. But getting more data can help. The data they referred to is available to us also on the Labor Department's web site. Here's a picture of it, expressed as open construction jobs as a percentage of total construction jobs (Figure 10.2):

Figure 10.2. The percent of unfilled construction jobs is in fact growing, albeit at a erratic pace. The headline was right!

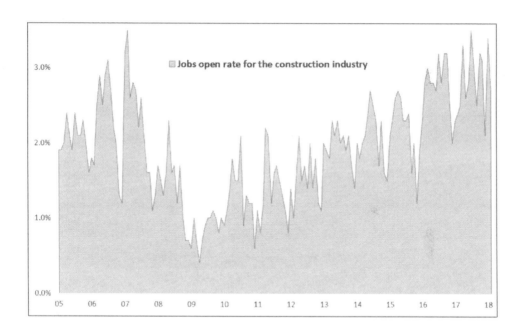

Example 4: China Debt

I REFERRED EARLIER TO CHINA'S CURRENT DEBT BUBBLE. If China has truly begun attacking its debt bubble, then a recession is in its future, which would be bad news for US GDP and bad for business profits. I therefore noted with interest this Bloomberg News headline on August 8, 2017: "China Is Taking on the 'Original Sin' of Its Mountain of Debt."

The first paragraph gave me hope that the article contained useful information:

China's much-vaunted campaign to tackle its leverage problem has captured headlines this year. But to understand why they're taking on the challenge—and the threat it could pose to the world's second-largest economy—you need to dig into the mountain.

That "digging into the mountain" seems promising, so let's see what the author's supporting evidence looks like. The best data in the article was in my favorite form, namely charts.

Figure 10.3, taken from the Bloomberg article, shows a history of *wealth management products* (WMPs) outstanding in China.

Figure 10.3. Growth rate of wealth management products (WMPs) in China. (Source: China Regulatory Banking Commission, cited by Bloomberg.)

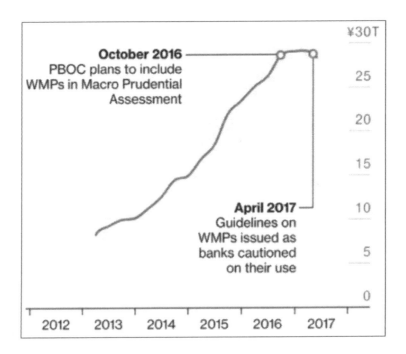

The article describes WMPs this way: "A way for borrowers who have trouble getting traditional bank loans to win funding . . ." The chart shows that growth in WMPs has leveled off, suggesting that China is having some success in restraining riskier debt growth.

Now let's turn to figure 10.4, also from the Bloomberg article. It shows a history of shadow banking assets, which are loans that don't appear on bank balance sheets. These are similar to the US asset-backed securities that I described earlier in the book, which were a major contributor to the over-lending that led to the 2008 financial crisis.

Figure 10.4. Growth of shadow banking assets in China. (Source: Bloomberg Intelligence.)

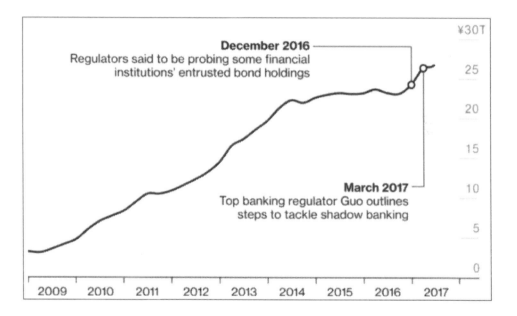

The chart shows that the growth of China's shadow banking assets has reaccelerated, arguing that regulators there had only mixed success at best in taming the country's debt bubble. It doesn't give much support to the headline that China is actively addressing its debt bubbles. So we have a case of mixed signals—WMPs flattening, but shadow banking assets still rising. I need more facts before I can feel comfortable that a trend has been established.

And sure enough, by the end of 2017, China's debt policy had changed. *The Wall Street Journal* reported that "bringing down debt, the priority for the past two years, is gone in favor of a pledge to just control the rise in borrowing" (December 19, 2017). Why? Because the government realized that bringing down debt would bring on bad economic times. Then on April 18, 2018, *The Wall Street Journal* reported that "China's central bank gave a green light to banks to dig into reserves to lend more, signaling government concern that rising trade tensiopns with the U.S. could slow the momentum of economic growth." So deferring a decision until stronger evidence surfaced turned out to be helpful.

The Payoff

WE'VE COME TO THE END OF OUR JOURNEY. We've tracked the ups and downs of our economic lives. We've shared some laughs, and, yes, some tears (I'm man enough to admit it). All in an effort to see if we can squeeze a little more growth out of our savings.

I hope I've convinced you that forecasting changes in the pace of debt growth in the US can improve your investment returns by helping you do a better job of shifting your asset allocation between cash, bonds, and stocks.

Of course, there are plenty of other approaches that attempt to improve investment returns. *Momentum investors* simply ride trends, assuming that what went up yesterday will go up today. *Day traders* try to anticipate minute-by-minute shifts in investor sentiment. *Value investors* try to identify individual securities they believe the market has materially mispriced. Acolytes of Warren Buffett buy companies they believe have sustainable advantages and hold them forever.

All of these investment strategies have their place; I even fancy myself as a value investor of individual stocks. Call me at 911 for some of my ideas.

But simple, well-timed shifts in asset allocation can yield important financial benefits. One last chart: Figure 10.5 shows the three-year forward returns on stocks and bonds, including interest and dividend payments.

Figure 10.5. The three-year forward returns (change in value plus interest and dividend payments) for stocks and bonds. (Sources: 1-year CD rate—Fed and FSLIC. 10-year Treasury bond—Fed. S&P 500 index—Yahoo Finance. S&P dividends—Stern Business School from Bloomberg.)

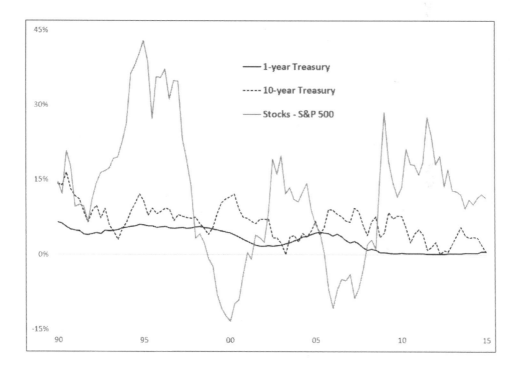

Wouldn't it have been nice to overweight stocks to take advantage of the three debt-induced stock market rallies in the 1980s, 1990s, and 2000s— as well as the debt/Federal Reserve rally in the 2010s that has persisted as of this writing? And to shift towards bonds in a timely fashion as those debt-induced stock booms inevitably imploded?

A brief history of my own investment odyssey may be instructive. In early 1987, I came up with the first version of my investment valuation model. The model said that, at the time, stocks were expensive. But the stock market kept rising, so late that summer I decided that my model was stupid, and I bought a bunch of stocks—just in time for the October, 1987, stock market crash!

Why do life lessons always require pain? What's the matter with "no pain, lots of gain"? But I digress.

During the 1990s, I was generally fully invested in stocks, although not in the tech stocks that were booming back then. There were plenty of days in 1998 and 1999 when I felt like a dope. I vividly remember being on a sales trip in San Francisco, with a driver for the day taking me to client appointments. I was pitching the idea that tech stocks were in a bubble and that the humble mortgage stocks I was following were a better bet—advice that most of my clients politely shrugged off. In those primitive days, my driver used my client time to trade Internet stocks over a pay phone. All in all, the situation felt pretty humiliating: I was getting ignored by my clients, while my driver was making money doing the opposite of what I recommended!

Of course, then came the crash in 2000 and 2001, when tech stocks nosedived, and my mortgage stocks did hold up well.

Out of the ashes of the tech implosion rose the housing bubble. By then, I had figured out the role of debt growth in the economy and investing. From 2004 on, I was telling clients that something bad was going to happen to mortgage debt, to housing, and to the stock market. In 2006, I began to act on my beliefs. I sold what I considered to be risky stocks and raised cash. I shorted a number of stocks particularly exposed to housing (that is, I placed a financial bet that those stocks would decline in value). And I kept a group of what I considered safe stocks. My only mistake was the last decision; many of those "safe" stocks turned out to be not so safe. But for 2008 as a whole, when the stock market declined by almost 40%, I was down about 10%.

As for today, being on the (ahem) older side, I should naturally have a more conservative asset allocation. And I do. But I do eat my own cooking, so today I am overweighted in stocks and cash and have nearly no bonds.

Most important, I keep watching for possible changes in the direction of debt growth. And for signs that the Federal Reserve will change its interest rate policies. I keep an eye out for the various influences on inflation: debt growth, labor costs, trade policy, and oil prices. So I do what I suggest in this book. I check out the government data. The days when quarterly releases of the Federal Reserve's Financial Accounts of the United States occur are periods of study and contemplation. I scan the newspaper and other media for anecdotes that point to changes in trends, asking questions like:

- Will the anti-immigration political movement gain enough momentum to really slow down US population growth and household formations?
- Is a regime change in Venezuela imminent, and what would that mean for oil prices?
- Is the labor market tightening up enough to force the Federal Reserve to start to seriously raise interest rates?
- Is bank regulation loosening up enough to make a difference in private-sector loan growth?

Each anecdote and data point adds to my mental data base, a very miniature version of the big data that many companies are now relying upon to analyze markets. That data base helps me continually monitor current trends in debt growth, Fed policy, inflation, and risk levels. It's rare that I spot a meaningful change in any of these trends. Trends don't change in minutes, they change over years, which means that a few data points encountered in my daily reading are unlikely to reflect a seismic shift. But if enough evidence emerges to suggest that some important trend is changing, I take advantage of the information by shifting my asset allocation accordingly.

It's a system that has served me well. I believe it can do the same for you.

Acknowledgments

FIRST AND ALWAYS, thanks to my wife Jamie and my two children, Matt and Liza. Not only do they give me constant joy, they patiently listened to my book stories without showing obvious boredom.

Thanks to my editor, Karl Weber, who helped me so much in big and small ways. To my publicist Fauzia Burke, for explaining the real modern book world to me. And to my brother-in-law Paul Golob, who gave me my first book-related advice and recommended Karl.

Thanks to my friends and readers, who all changed the book for the better in some fashion—Karen Zimmerman, John Cecil, Steve Shapiro, Mark Altman, Andy Rodman, Tom Fogarty, Barbara Steiner, Larry Jeydel, Jack Gorman, Neal Keller, Tom Zimmerman, Dr. Alex Mauskopf, Steve Rosenblatt, Stuart Katz, Mitch Weisberg, Susan Feitler, the Reverend Bill Damrow, and Tom Silver.

Thanks to my employers over the years, who paid me money for learning—Merrill Lynch, EF Hutton, PaineWebber (a special shout-out), UBS, Annaly Capital, and Portales Partners.

As a retired bum, I now collect my own data and create my own charts, but it wasn't always so. Many of the first charts were initiated by the talented assistants who worked with me over the years. So thank you, Alison Williams, Ragen Stienke, Tom Fogarty, and Bose George.

Thanks to my writing venues. My libraries—Mamaroneck, Larchmont, and the beautiful rooms in New York's Bryant Park library. My patio, which provided both a lovely spot to write and a chance to study squirrel and neighbor behavior.

Thanks to the nameless and faceless public servants who collected the data that is the heart of this book. Here's to you guys and gals at the Federal Reserve, the Bureau of Economic Analysis, the Labor Department, the Census Bureau and elsewhere. Those numbers are good, right?

A shout out to my computer, an Asus laptop with Intel and Windows inside. Where would we be without Word and Excel?

And finally, thanks to you, dear reader, for giving my ideas a chance. Hopefully you learned something, and had a bit of fun along the way.

Gary Gordon
June, 2018

Index

About the Author

GARY GORDON SPENT HIS career at Paine Webber, UBS, and other Wall Street firms, where he was a stock analyst covering the housing, mortgage, and consumer finance industries. He also served as a US investment strategist and as a portfolio manager.

Gordon is an adjunct professor in the math department at Mercy College. He teaches at prisons (Sing Sing and Taconic in New York) and tutors in a junior high school. He also presents financial literacy seminars to adults and students. He serves on the Board of Hudson Link, which is dedicated to providing college education to incarcerated men and women, and on an operating committee at the United Jewish Appeal.

Gordon is married with two young adult children. He has degrees from Colgate University (BA 1974, philosophy) and The Wharton School (MBA 1977, finance).

92880048R00132

Made in the USA
Lexington, KY
11 July 2018